IWO JIMA

DEDICATION

This work is dedicated to the Marines, sailors, airmen, soldiers and Coast Guardsmen who gave their lives or suffered grievously to wrest control of Iwo Jima from the Japanese to assist in bringing the hellacious Pacific War closer to its conclusion.

IWO JIMA
THE MARINE CORPS' EPIC VICTORY

JON DIAMOND

Pen & Sword
MILITARY

First published in Great Britain in 2025 by
PEN & SWORD MILITARY
an imprint of Pen & Sword Books Ltd
Yorkshire – Philadelphia

ISBN 978-1-03610-714-7

Typeset by Concept, Huddersfield, West Yorkshire, HD4 5JL
Printed and bound in England by CPI Group (UK) Ltd, Croydon, CR0 4YY

Pen & Sword Books Limited incorporates the imprints of Archaeology, Atlas,
Aviation, Discovery, Family History, Fiction, History, Maritime, Military,
Military Classics, Politics, Select, Transport, True Crime, Air World,
Frontline Publishing, Leo Cooper, Remember When, Seaforth Publishing,
The Praetorian Press, Wharncliffe Local History, Wharncliffe Transport,
Wharncliffe True Crime and White Owl.

For a complete list of Pen & Sword titles please contact
PEN & SWORD BOOKS LTD
47 Church Street, Barnsley, South Yorkshire, S70 2AS, England
E-mail: enquiries@pen-and-sword.co.uk
Website: www.pen-and-sword.co.uk
or
PEN & SWORD BOOKS
1950 Lawrence Rd, Havertown, PA 19083, USA
E-mail: uspen-and-sword@casematepublishers.com
Website: www.penandswordbooks.com

Contents

Foreword

'The raising of that flag on Suribachi means a Marine Corps for the next 500 years,' said James Forrestal, Secretary of the Navy, on 23 February 1945. The United States Marine Corps is known throughout the United States Armed Forces for its high standards, unrelenting discipline and, above all, *esprit de corps*. From the first moments of recruit training, United States Marines are instilled with a combination of reverence and awe for the feats of valor accomplished by those Marines who came before them. In the vernacular of Marines, difficult challenges are often compared to the famous battles and engagements in which Marines have emerged victorious; but the one comparison reserved for the most sacred of occasions is the capture of Mount Suribachi.

On 23 February 1945, Joe Rosenthal captured the photo that would become the most iconic representation of the United States Marine Corps. The flag raising on Mount Suribachi is commemorated in countless monuments, pins, magnets and posters, and served as the inspiration for the design of the National Museum of the Marine Corps in Quantico, Virginia. For Marines, the flag raising on Iwo Jima represents a reputation earned through the blood and sacrifice of their predecessors, a reputation that demands no less sacrifice from any who would join the ranks of the world's finest fighting force.

Although Secretary of the Navy James Forrestal's prediction has yet to be proven true, ask any Marine, and they will tell you that 500 years doesn't even come close.

Captain Shawn Taylor,
United States Marine Corps Reserve

Acknowledgements

As a book, there would be no memorialization of this thirty-six-day campaign if not for the combat photographers who took the images under fire, suffering wounds and even dying. Where identifiable, the names of these photographers appear next to the source of the photograph.

The author is indebted to the skilled archivists at the Still Photo Section, National Archives and Records Administration (NARA) II; the History Division at the United States Marine Corps University (USMCU); and the United States Army Heritage and Education Center (USAHEC) for their helpful assistance.

Maps in Chapter 5 are from Lt Col Whitman S. Bartley, USMC, *Iwo Jima: Amphibious Epic* (Washington, DC: Historical Branch G-3 Division, Headquarters Marine Corps, 1954).

Abbreviations

AA – Anti-aircraft
AAA – Anti-aircraft artillery
ADC – Aide-de-Camp
AIF – Australian Imperial Force
AP – Armour-piercing
AT – Anti-tank
BAR – Browning Automatic Rifle
BG – Bomb Group
Capt – Captain
CB – Construction Battalion
CD – Coastal Defence
CG – Commanding General
C-in-C – Commander-in-Chief
CINCPOA – Commander-in-Chief, Pacific Ocean Area
CINPAC – Commander-in-Chief, Pacific Fleet
CNO – Chief of Naval Operations
CO – Commanding Officer
COMINCH – Commander-in-Chief, US Fleet
COS – Chief of Staff
CP – Command Post
CPA – Central Pacific Area
Cpl – Corporal
DP – Dual-purpose
DSC – Distinguished Service Cross
DUKW – Manufacturer code with 'D' as model year, 1942; 'U' referring to body style, utility (amphibious); 'K' for all-wheel drive; and 'W' for dual rear axles
ETO – European Theatre of Operations
FA – Field Artillery
G-1 – Personnel Officer
G-2 – Intelligence Officer

G-3 – Operations Officer
G-4 – Logistics Officer
G-5 – Plans Officer
G – General Motors
GMC – General Motors Corporation
HE – High Explosive
HMC – Howitzer Motor Carriage
HMG – Heavy Machine Gun
IIIAC – III Amphibious Corps
IJA – Imperial Japanese Army
IJN – Imperial Japanese Navy
IJNAF – Imperial Japanese Naval Air Force
IMAC – I Marine Amphibious Corps
IMB – Independent Mixed Brigade
IR – Infantry Regiment
JCS – Joint Chiefs of Staff
KIA – Killed in action
LC – Lieutenant Colonel
LCI – Landing Craft, Infantry
LCM – Landing Craft, Mechanized
LCT – Landing Craft, Tank
LCVP – Landing Craft Vehicle and Personnel
LG – Lieutenant General
LMG – Light Machine Gun
LSD – Landing Ship, dock
LSM – Landing Ship, Medium
LST – Landing Ship, Tank
MG – Machine Gun
MIA – Missing in Action
MIS – Military Intelligence Service
MMG – Medium Machine Gun
NARA – National Archives and Records Administration
NCO – Non-Commissioned Officer

NEI – Netherlands East Indies
NLF – Naval Landing Force
OP – Observation Post
Pfc – Private 1st Class
POA – Pacific Ocean Areas
PTO – Pacific Theatre of Operations
QF – Quick-firing
RAdm – Rear Admiral
SMG – Submachine Gun
SNLF – Special Naval Landing Force
SPA – South Pacific Area
SSgt – Staff Sergeant
SWPA – Southwest Pacific Area
TB – Tank Battalion
TBF – Torpedo Bomber Fighter
(Grumman)

TF – Task Force
TSgt – Technical Sergeant
USAAF – United States Army Air
Forces
USAHEC – United States Army
Heritage and Education Center
USMC – United States Marine Corps
USN – United States Navy
VAdm – Vice Admiral
VAC – Fifth Amphibious Corps
WIA – Wounded in Action
WO – Warrant Officer
WP – White Phosphorus
XO – Executive Officer

Chapter One

Strategic Prelude to the Invasion of Iwo Jima, 19 February 1945

General Curtis LeMay was sent by General Henry Arnold, CG, USAAF, to improve the proficiency of the 21st Bomb Group in the Marianas. Bad weather and high winds over Japanese targets on Honshu were posed as reasons for the B-29 Superfortress's failure to bring Japan to its knees in October 1944 when the raids initially began. However, another major factor was the increasing number of Japanese fighters that sortied from Iwo Jima and disrupted the B-29 tight formations when the bombers passed over the Volcano Islands, where radar stations warned Tokyo of the raids. One of LeMay's first tasks was to neutralize the Japanese fighter presence on Iwo Jima. He also regarded the island as a useful refuelling and emergency strip for crippled bombers midway between Japan and the Marianas (see map, p. 4). LeMay told Admiral Spruance, the Fifth Fleet CO, at a January 1945 Saipan conference that 'without Iwo Jima I couldn't bomb Japan effectively'. Nimitz, as early as September 1943, was ordered by Washington's Joint War Planning Committee to seize enemy-held islands in the Bonin, Volcano and Ryukyu Islands.

Iwo Jima was the most heavily fortified enemy Pacific island site to defend its two well-constructed air bases, which enabled Japan to base their fighter squadrons to interdict the westward American advance across the Central Pacific Ocean towards the East China Sea (see map, p. 4). A third airfield further north was under construction. The American High Command wanted Iwo Jima's airfields to base P-51 fighter escorts to accompany the Mariana-based B-29 bombers as they pounded the Japanese Home Islands, and to provide emergency landing fields for damaged Superfortresses that were suffering heavy losses on their 2,500-mile round trip from Tinian and Saipan to bomb Japanese cities and military installations. Allied planners believed that the American occupation of Iwo Jima would deal a psychological blow to Japanese morale as the island was traditionally viewed as Nipponese territory administered from Tokyo. For these reasons, the Marine Corps was to embark on one of its most bitter, yet epic, campaigns of the Pacific War.

After completion of the final rehearsals, Major General Harry Schmidt's VAC landing force, comprised of the 4th and 5th Divisions, was anchored off Saipan on 14–15 February 1945. While en route to Iwo Jima, for D-Day on 19 February, the VAC assault force was provided air cover from the US Fifth Fleet carrier force and protection by naval surface vessels. Due to Iwo's distance from Japanese Home Island airfields, Spruance's Fifth Fleet carriers were spared from numerous *kamikaze* attacks. One attack did occur on 21 February and damaged the USS *Saratoga* and the escort carrier USS *Bismarck Sea*.

Before Marines amphibiously assaulted Iwo Jima, the island was subjected to the longest and most intensive bombardment preparation given to any objective during the Pacific War (see pp. 12–16). From the initial USN carrier raid of June 1944 on Iwo Jima to the pre-H-Hour bombardment of 19 February, tons of explosives rained down on the small island's airfields and installations. The Japanese defenders survived the 20,000 rounds of heavy naval shells and the thousands of tons of bombs dropped from B-24 heavy bombers from Saipan.

The triumvirate of USN commanders that led naval and Marine forces throughout the Pacific campaigns stand in front of a B-24 Liberator on Saipan during the summer of 1944. From left to right are Admiral Raymond A. Spruance, Admiral Ernest J. King, COMINCH and CNO (a dual posting solely held by him), and Admiral Chester W. Nimitz, CINCPAC and CINCPOA. On 5 August 1943, Spruance was placed in command of the CPA with its redesignated Fifth Fleet on 29 April 1944 and would lead it during the invasion and ensuing ground combat on Iwo Jima, Operation DETACH-MENT, commencing on 19 February 1945. Spruance worked well with Rear Admiral Richmond Kelly Turner, the Fifth Fleet's amphibious force CO. Admiral King, a fleet admiral during the Second World War, directing the USN operations, planning and administration while also serving as a member of the US JCS. Admiral Nimitz, a naval authority on submarines, took over command of the Pacific Fleet after Pearl Harbor, becoming an admiral on 31 December 1941, and was in charge of POA beginning 24 March 1942, being promoted to fleet admiral on 19 December 1944. Nimitz stated during the Iwo Jima campaign, 'Among the Americans who served on Iwo Jima, uncommon valour was a common virtue.' (*NARA*)

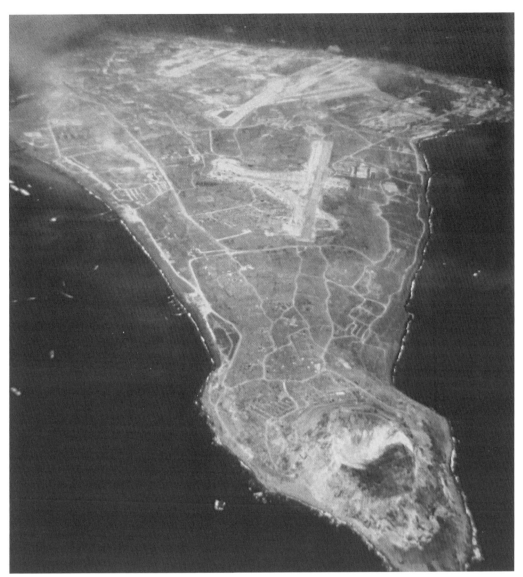

Iwo Jima aerial view with the highest point, Mount Suribachi (variably listed as 546 to 556 feet), an extinct volcano, seen at the island's southern end (right foreground). Airfield No. 1 nearest Mount Suribachi was constructed in 1943 by the IJN as an intermediate aircraft base from Japan to the Mariana Islands, as well as an airbase to protect Japanese convoys. During 1944, a second airfield (north of Airfield No. 1) became operational and construction was begun on a third strip at the island's northern end (left background). In February 1944, there were only 1,500 IJNAF personnel and twenty aircraft on the island. The next month, Iwo Jima's garrison was increased to 3,000 IJA and 2,000 IJN personnel. After Truk in the Caroline Islands was raided by Spruance's carriers in February 1944 and the IJN's Combined Fleet retired from that anchorage, Iwo Jima acquired defensive strategic importance for the Home Islands. The main objective of the 19 February 1945 Marine invasion (Operation DETACHMENT) was seizure of the Iwo Jima airfields for American fighter aircraft to escort B-29 Superfortresses on their Mariana Islands-based raids on the Japanese Home Islands and to provide an emergency airfield for the damaged or fuel-depleted heavy bombers to land that would otherwise have had to crash into the sea. The major eastern shore landing beaches for the Marines on 19 February were proximate to Airfield No. 1, the main objective of D-Day. (NARA)

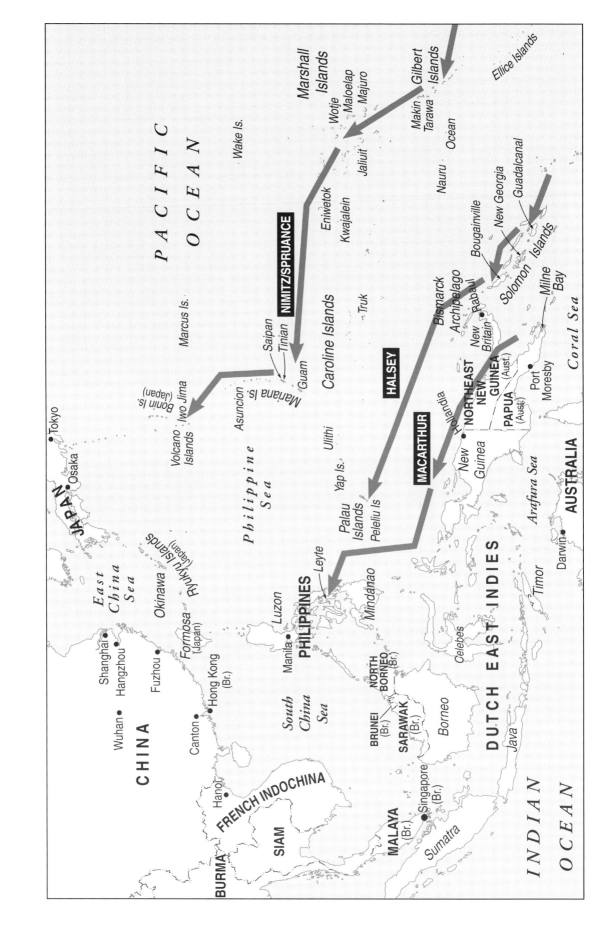

A map shows the Allied Counteroffensive Axes in the Central (Nimitz/Spruance), South (Halsey) and Southwest Pacific (MacArthur) Areas of Operation, 1942–45. Vice Admiral Raymond Spruance, formerly Nimitz's COS, commanded the CPA campaigns involving USN, Marine and Army forces advancing in separate hotly contested invasions of the Gilbert Islands (November 1943), the Marshall Islands (January–February 1944) and the Mariana Islands (June–August 1944) prior to Iwo Jima's invasion on 19 February 1945. Admiral Halsey was given command of the tenuous Guadalcanal campaign in October 1942, and after the Japanese evacuation in early February 1943, he led the Allied forces in the SPA for the drive up the Central Solomons (including New Georgia Island) through to Bougainville in the northern part of the island chain throughout 1943. In May 1944, Halsey was promoted to CO of the newly formed Third Fleet, leading the naval campaigns to take the Palau islands, Leyte and Luzon, and later raid the Japanese Home Islands. General Douglas A. MacArthur, CO SWPA, led his US and Australian ground forces, Lieutenant General George Kenney's Allied Air Forces and 5th USAAF, and USN's Seventh Fleet, under Vice Admiral Thomas Kinkaid, and Rear Admiral Daniel Barbey's VII Amphibious Force, driving along the northern coast of North-East and Netherlands New Guinea, western New Britain at Cape Gloucester and Arawe, and the Admiralty Islands invasion, all in 1943–44 as a prelude to assault Leyte in October 1944 and Luzon in December 1944. (*Meridian Mapping*)

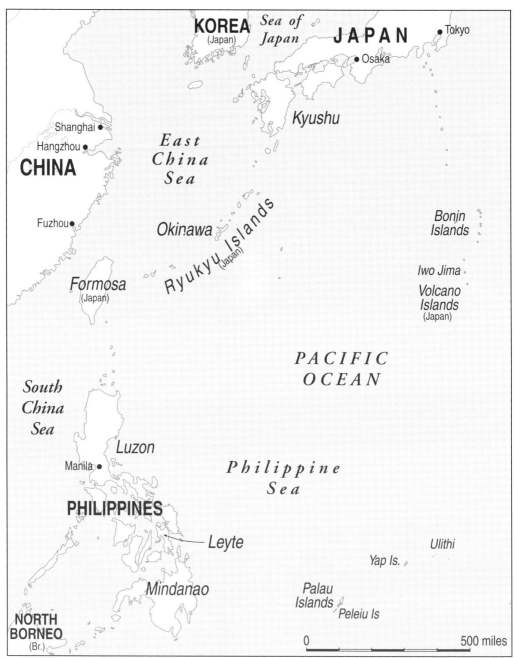

(**Above**) The pertinent Pacific War campaign locales from September 1944 to April 1945. In mid-1944, MacArthur's SWPA ground and naval forces were ordered to liberate the Philippines beginning in October 1944 at Leyte. To secure MacArthur's eastern flank at Leyte, Halsey's Third Fleet attacked Peleliu in the Palau group of the western Caroline Islands, directly due east of Mindanao, on 15 September 1944. Leyte was invaded by General Walter Krueger's Sixth Army's X and XXIV Corps on 20 October 1944 with the transport and protection of Admiral Halsey's Third and Kinkaid's Seventh Fleets. MacArthur declared major combat operations on Leyte completed on 25 December.

The final major liberation campaign for the Philippines started with the invasion of Luzon at Lingayen Gulf by the Sixth Army's I and XIV Corps on 9 January 1945. Bataan (16 February), Corregidor (2 March) and Manila (4 March) were all reclaimed by MacArthur's forces, although it was not to be until 5 July that the SWPA commander announced the Philippines' final liberation. After the seizure of the Marianas, Nimitz was ordered to seize Iwo Jima on 19 February 1945, located in the Volcano Islands just south of the Bonin Island chain and midway between Japan and the Mariana Islands. By 7 April, the P-51 fighters were able to fly escort for the B-29s. Also, Iwo Jima provided emergency landing fields for damaged Superfortresses beginning on 4 March. (*Meridian Mapping*)

(**Below**) Two North American long-range P-51 Mustang fighters of USAAF's VII Fighter Command taxi down Airfield No. 1 on 15 March 1945, with Mount Suribachi to the south in the background, for a raid on Chichi Jima in the Bonin Islands, 155 miles to the north. In addition to sorties in the Volcano and Bonin Islands, the P-51s provided escort coverage for the B-29 Superfortresses during their Mariana Islands-based Japan raids. (*NARA*)

(**Above**) Three B-29 Superfortresses fly in formation from their Mariana Islands XXI Bomber Command bases to raid Japan. The heroic sacrifice in bloodshed that the Marines made in their capture of Iwo Jima from 19 February to 26 March 1945 enabled 2,251 B-29 emergency landings beginning on 4 March, saving 24,771 airmen. On 7 April, 100 P-51 Mustangs escorted the B-29s on a daylight raid over Japan and more Japanese aircraft than American ones were shot down, a tally pattern that was to persist, and more importantly, lowered bomber losses to below 5 per cent. Bomber crews became demoralized at losses above 5 per cent since it translated into an average expectancy of about sixteen raids before a B-29 with its crew was lost to enemy interception. (*NARA*)

(**Opposite**) The USAAF's VII Fighter Command's last major raid for May 1945 was a daylight incendiary attack against Yokohama on 29 May, when 101 P-51s escorted 517 B-29s. This USAAF raid was intercepted by 150 A6M Reisen 'Zero' fighters, resulting in a major air duel in which 5 B-29s were shot down and another 175 damaged. The P-51 pilots claimed twenty-six 'Zeroes' shot down, with another twenty-three 'probables', for the loss of three American fighters. On 1 June, 521 B-29s escorted by 148 P-51s were dispatched in a daylight raid against Osaka. Unfortunately, thick clouds complicated the mission, resulting in twenty-seven P-51s destroyed in collisions. Nevertheless, 458 B-29s and their remaining fighter escort reached Osaka. Other attacks in June were on Kobe (5 June), and Osaka again (7 and 15 June). The 15 June raid marked the end of the first phase of General Curtis LeMay's XXI Bomber Command's attacks on Japanese cities.

Despite the P-51 escort, 136 B-29s were downed during the campaign, underscoring the importance of an emergency landing strip on Iwo Jima. P-51s also conducted a series of independent ground-attack missions against targets in the Japanese Home Islands between 26 April and 22 June. Due to the lack of Japanese aerial interdiction by enemy fighters during the B-29 raids in July 1945, VII Fighter Command was tasked with ground-attack missions from then on against airfields, to destroy enemy aircraft reserved for *kamikaze* attacks on the anticipated USN invasion fleet during Operation OLYPMPIC, the assault on the southern Japanese island of Kyushu slated for 1 December 1945. By the end of the war, VII Fighter Command conducted fifty-one ground-attack raids on Japanese targets. USAAF losses were 91 fighter pilots killed and 157 P-51s destroyed during these missions. (*NARA*)

(**Above**) A damaged B-29 Superfortress 'crash-landed' on Iwo Jima at Airfield No. 1 after a raid on Tokyo on 10 March 1945. The shell-holed volcanic ash is visible (foreground). On 4 March, the B-29 *Dinah Might* preceded the above 'crash-landing' and was the first Superfortress to use Iwo Jima's Airfield No. 1 as an emergency strip, when it was low on fuel and badly shot up during its return flight to its Tinian base in the Marianas. (*NARA*)

(**Opposite**) A map shows Iwo Jima's Japanese defences prepared from ground study from 19 February to 19 March 1945. Airfields Nos. 1 and 2 are visible in the southern and central parts of the island, with the incomplete Airfield No. 3 north of Motoyama Village and the sulphur mine refinery just to the south of the rugged hill and ridge terrain of the northern portion of Iwo Jima. The vast array of ordnance positions, casemates, block-houses and shelters, among other sites (listed in the legend), housed the ninety-five 75mm AA guns used in an AT role that were extremely effective, along with landmines, to destroy many Marine tanks and amphibious tractors at the beachhead and inland. By 1 February 1945, Kuribayashi had over 360 artillery pieces of 75mm or larger-calibre, twelve 320mm spigot mortars, sixty-five medium (155mm) and light (81mm) mortars, and thirty-three naval guns of 80mm or larger. In addition, there were more than 200 20mm and 25mm AA guns and seventy 37mm and 47mm AT guns. The Japanese had seventy rocket guns and crews using either 8-inch rockets weighing 200lb that could travel 2,000–3,000 yards or an enormous 550lb projectile with a 7,500-yard range. Colonel Nishi had over a score of tanks, of the Ha-Go and Chi-Ha type, under his command. The 204th Naval Construction battalion's 1,200 members constructed pillboxes and other fortifications. In early August 1944, 2,000 naval personnel including aviators and ground crews arrived. On D-Day, 19 February 1945, the total Japanese garrison exceeded 21,000 troops (IJA 15,500 and IJN 5,500), far exceeding American intelligence estimates. The Marine eastern landing beaches are shown extending from just north of Mount Suribachi to the East Boat Basin. The major Japanese defensive sectors were the Mount Suribachi one at the island's southern end. The Western sector was between Motoyama Airfields Nos. 1 and 2. The Southern sector was situated to the south-east of Airfield No. 2, while the eastern sector was located in the north-eastern end of the island, defended mainly with IJN troops. The Northern sector extended to the island's northern tip at Kitano Point, where Lieutenant General Kuribayashi had his final redoubt. (*NARA*)

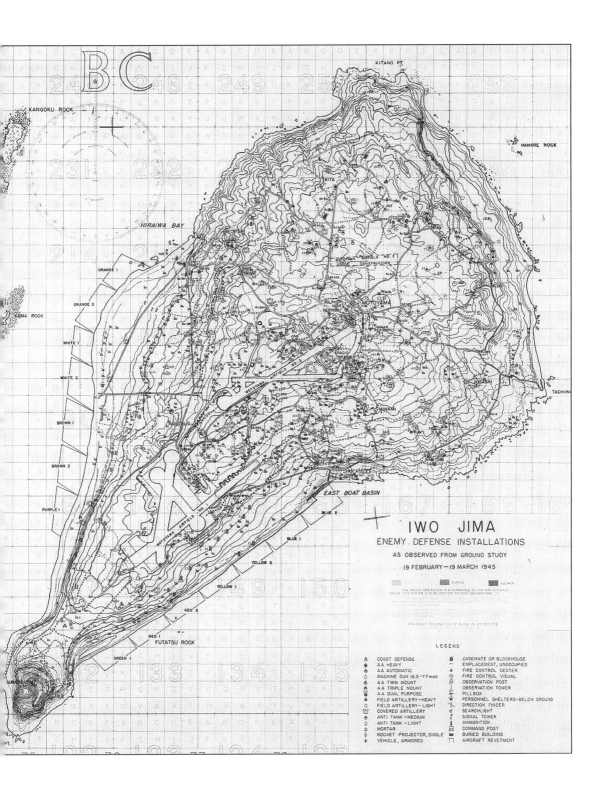

KITANO PT

KANGOKU ROCK

HANARE ROCK

HIRAIWA BAY

KITA

ORANGE 1

ORANGE 2

KAMA ROCK

MOTOYAMA AIRFIELD NO. 3
UNDER CONSTRUCTION

MOTOYAMA

WHITE 1

WHITE 2

MOTOYAMA AIRFIELD NO. 2

HIGASHI

TACHIIWA

MINAMI

BROWN 1

BROWN 2

EAST BOAT BASIN

PURPLE 1

BLUE 2

BLUE 1

MOTOYAMA AIRFIELD NO. 1

YELLOW 2

IWO JIMA
ENEMY DEFENSE INSTALLATIONS
AS OBSERVED FROM GROUND STUDY
19 FEBRUARY—19 MARCH 1945

PURPLE   SALMON

THE SPECIAL GRID SYSTEM IS SUPERIMPOSED ON THIS MAP IN PURPLE
COLOR. THIS SYSTEM IS TO BE USED FOR PIN-POINT DESIGNATIONS.

PIN-POINT DESIGNATION OF R-164 IS BO 750-709

YELLOW 1

RED 2

RED 1
FUTATSU ROCK

GREEN 1

LEGEND

	COAST DEFENSE		CASEMATE OR BLOCKHOUSE
	A A HEAVY		EMPLACEMENT, UNOCCUPIED
	A A AUTOMATIC		FIRE CONTROL CENTER
	MACHINE GUN (6.5-7.7 mm)		FIRE CONTROL VISUAL
	A A TWIN MOUNT		OBSERVATION POST
	A A TRIPLE MOUNT		OBSERVATION TOWER
	A A DUAL PURPOSE		PILLBOX
	FIELD ARTILLERY—HEAVY		PERSONNEL SHELTERS—BELOW GROUND
	FIELD ARTILLERY—LIGHT		DIRECTION FINDER
	COVERED ARTILLERY		SEARCHLIGHT
	ANTI TANK—MEDIUM		SIGNAL TOWER
	ANTI TANK—LIGHT		AMMUNITION
	MORTAR		COMMAND POST
	ROCKET PROJECTOR, SINGLE		BURIED BUILDING
	VEHICLE, ARMORED		AIRCRAFT REVETMENT

11

(**Above**) B-24 Liberator four-engine heavy bombers of the 7th USAAF raid Iwo Jima's Airfield No. 1 laden with Japanese aircraft, in mid-June 1944. About 100 IJN aircraft were destroyed during this initial 15 June raid by the 7th USAAF's 11th and 30th BGs operating from the Mariana Islands. The 494th BG operated from the Palau Islands after their capture in November 1944. At this time, there were few defensive fortifications on the island. (*NARA*)

(**Opposite, above**) A four-engine B-24 Liberator heavy bomber of the 7th USAAF flies away from Iwo's western shoreline after enemy defences were bombed in a February 1945 raid. Mount Suribachi (right), the island's the highest point, is at the southern end. The USAAF conducted seventy-four consecutive days of bombing raids on Iwo Jima beginning 8 December 1944, to weaken Japanese defences before the 19 February amphibious assault. The workhorses of the air assaults on Iwo Jima were the four-engine heavy B-24 Liberator bombers of the 7th USAAF stationed in the Mariana Islands, marking the greatest effort made by this unit in the Pacific. (*NARA*)

(**Opposite, below**) B-24 Liberator heavy bombers of the 7th USAAF drop their bombs on Japanese AA sites between Airfield No. 1 (centre left) and Airfield No. 2 (foreground) in October 1944. Air missions before 31 January 1945 numbered up to thirty to forty sorties daily. Marine B-25 medium bombers (designated PBJs) of VMB-612 also participated in Iwo Jima's bombing from early December 1944 until 31 January 1945. These Marine aircraft operated from the Marianas under VII Bomber Command and flew night missions through the Volcano Islands as the IJN was frantically trying to supply Iwo Jima's outposts during nocturnal hours. Using rockets and radar, twenty-three IJN ships were sunk by the Marine aircraft. (*NARA*)

54723 A

(**Opposite, above**) A B-24 Liberator heavy bomber of the 7th USAAF drops seven 55-gallon fuel drums as fire bombs on Airfield No. 1 on 1 February 1945. Plywood fins were used as stabilizers on the fuel drums to replace unavailable metal ones. (*NARA*)

(**Opposite, below**) Black clouds of billowing smoke emanate from Airfield No. 1 during a 7th USAAF bombing raid by B-24 Liberator heavy bombers. Note the wrecked Japanese aircraft piled at the edge of the runway (middle right). (*NARA*)

(**Above**) The battleship USS *New York* (BB-34), which entered service in 1915, bombards Iwo Jima with its five twin 14-inch and twenty-one single 5-inch guns on 16 February 1945. The island was divided into bombardment sectors from 16 to 17 February. The USS *New York*'s zone was in the centre of the island in the vicinity of Airfield No. 2. The *New York* was joined by the USS *Idaho*, *Tennessee*, *Nevada*, *Texas* and *Arkansas*, all arriving at Iwo Jima on 16 February for three days of pre-invasion bombardment to neutralize Japanese guns capable of hitting the invasion beaches. The *New York* fired 6,417 rounds, including 1,037 14-inch rounds, with one of its salvoes hitting a primary Japanese ammunition dump and creating a tremendous explosion. The USN bombardment of Iwo Jima commenced in November 1944 and continued with intervals until 16 February 1945. On 17 February, LCI gunboats and rocket boats manoeuvred close to shore to cover USN frogmen clearing the approaches and checking surf conditions. (*NARA*)

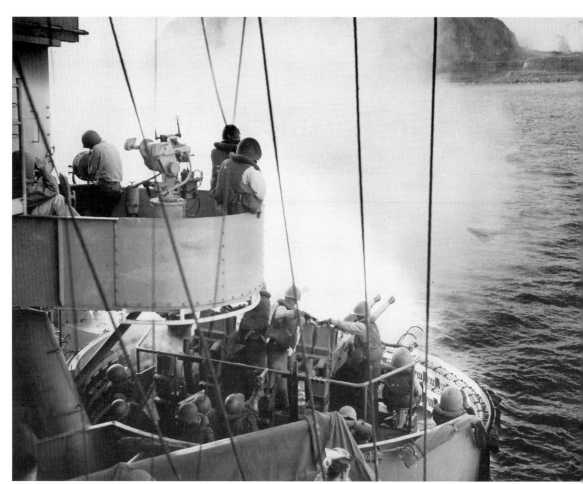

On D-Day, 19 February 1945, twin-barrelled 40mm Bofors AA guns in a quad mount on a USN battleship pound the southernmost landing beaches and beyond near Mount Suribachi (background). The naval AA guns could realistically fire sixty to ninety HE rounds per minute per barrel, since the weapon was manually loaded, with an effective range of 4,000 yards. (*NARA*)

Chapter Two

Terrain, Fortifications and Weapons

Iwo Jima, in the Volcano Islands, south of the Bonin Island chain, is 660 nautical miles south of Tokyo Bay and 625 nautical miles north-west of Saipan. Translated into English, Iwo Jima means 'Sulphur Island', derived from the sulphur deposits that extend to the very surface of the island. Sulphur vapours permeate the entire area, making for a ghostly landscape, with the ground itself being hot. The Japanese inhabitants of Iwo Jima, before the invasion, lived in five villages in the northern part of the island: Kita, Nishi, Motoyama, Higashi and Minami. An absence of potable water, other than rain, was logistically problematic given Iwo Jima's subtropical weather.

Mount Suribachi, an extinct volcano, forms the southern tip of the island and rises to 550 feet as the highest elevation. Iwo Jima measures 4.6 miles northeast-to-southwest, with a width varying from 2.5 miles to less than half a mile at the volcano's narrow base – a surface area of 7.5 square miles. Iwo's landing beaches north of the volcano were covered by deep, coarse, black volcanic ash forming 15-foot sand terraces that shifted over time in size and location from perpetual wave action of storms, impeding infantry and vehicular beach egress. The northern plateau's 1-mile diameter was comprised of steep rocky ridges, gorges, crevices, ravines and cliffs, the latter ascending directly from the water's edge, and had several elevations – the highest, Hill 382, located to the east of Airfield No. 2 between Motoyama and Minami villages. There were three other hills 362 feet in height, designated 362-A, 362-B and 362-C, as well as Hill 199 OBOE and Hill PETER. The island's desolation of sparse vegetation was accentuated by scrubwood. Throughout this terrain, the Japanese were entrenched in hundreds of natural and man-made caves.

For nine months prior to the 19 February 1945 amphibious Marine invasion, Lieutenant General Tadamichi Kuribayashi, the island's CG, utilized 25 per cent of his garrison supplemented with Korean labourers to construct massive above and below ground defences including tunnels, caves, artillery casemates, block-houses, bunkers, pillboxes and revetted tank positions, all with interconnected, mutually supporting fields of fire. These durably constructed defences and shelters withstood weeks of American naval and aerial bombardment. Some tunnels were more than 70 feet underground, extending interconnected in all directions with illumination to comprise a labyrinth. Most tunnels were 5 feet in height and 5 feet wide with concreted walls and ceilings, and hid supplies, ammunition and hospitals, and served as escape routes for Japanese troops isolated after the capture of the Mount Suribachi area to get to Iwo Jima's northern sector. The tunnels had variable levels to assure good ventilation and minimize the effect of bombs or shells exploding near the entrances or exits, as well as from the sulphur fumes present in many of the underground installations. Underground positions could hold 300 men, with multiple entrances and exits to prevent being trapped in any one cave. Iwo Jima's black volcanic ash could be converted into concrete when mixed with cement to reinforce some defences to 4 feet in thickness.

(**Opposite, above**) During the Mount Suribachi assault on 20 February 1945, a USN Grumman TBF Avenger carrier torpedo bomber flies overhead as 5th TB M4A3s advance towards the volcano base (background) and a Marine is near his 37mm AT gun (foreground). Major General Keller Rockey, 5th Division CG, assigned Colonel Harry Liversedge's 28th Marines to isolate and capture the volcano, codenamed HOTROCKS, from a USN map reference. (Photo: *Pvt R. Campbell*) (*NARA*)

(**Opposite, below**) A telephoto lens view of the American beachhead on 27 February 1945 as viewed from Mount Suribachi, which was captured by the 28th Marines, 5th Division four days previously. The beaches received a continuous stream of supplies and vehicles unloaded from LSTs, LSMs, LCMs, LCIs and other assault transports (naval identification numbers on the bows), often under ceaseless Japanese artillery, rocket and mortar fire. Bulldozed sand terraces enabled trucks, LVTs and DUKWs to move inland towards the Marine front lines. (Photo: *SSgt M. Kauffman*) (*NARA*)

(**Below**) Marine Pfc in 28th Marines, 5th Division looks over steaming sulphur beds that Japanese engineers had to ventilate from the tunnels to the surface. (*NARA*)

(**Above**) A Marine assault wave of the 2nd Battalion, 27th Marines (under the command of Colonel Thomas B. Wornham), 5th Division tries to overcome a 15-foot sand terrace by crawling slowly upwards inland from Red Beach 1 on 19 February 1945 as the smoke of the shore's bombardment and Japanese artillery fire drifts above them in their assault towards the southern end of Airfield No. 1. The soft volcanic ash impeded a rifleman with full kit from moving forward, along with land mines exploding on the terraces after Marines detonated them. Beyond the protection of this first high sand terrace, Marines received intense machine-gun and rifle fire from sand hummocks and pillboxes with barely visible apertures just above ground level; mortar rounds from well-concealed pits; blockhouses with heavy artillery; rapid-firing AA guns lowered to rake the beaches; and cave entrances and casemates from Suribachi's base and slopes housing large-calibre CD guns and mortars. Despite heavy casualties, by twilight the 5th Division units were digging in along the edge of Airstrip No. 1. (Photo: *Sgt J.T. Dreyfuss*) (*NARA*)

(**Opposite, above**) Marine stretcher cases are carried by Navy corpsmen and stretcher-bearers while 'walking wounded' trudge through the deep, soft volcanic sand towards an LST for evacuation. Those waiting evacuation at the beachhead, on 19 February 1945, moved past the smouldering wreckage of boats, supplies, equipment, and the bodies of fellow Marines, all in range of pre-sighted Japanese artillery. More than 1,000 casualties were evacuated before darkness, but hundreds remained on the beach. During the invasion's initial eighteen hours, 2,312 Marines had fallen. (Photo: *TSgt G.B. Kress*) (*NARA*)

(**Opposite, below**) Another view of the B-29 Superfortress resting in the volcanic sand after crash-landing near Airfield No. 1's runway after the 10 March 1945 Tokyo Raid. A P-51 Mustang, ground crew personnel, and a truck are on the runway. (*NARA*)

(**Above**) A Marine engineer demolition team sets off Japanese mines and 'booby traps' at the beachhead with a nearby bulldozer and a 1941 GMC CCKW 2.5-ton 6 × 6 truck with its 0.30-inch calibre LMG pointing upwards. Almost 570,000 CCKW trucks were built from 1941 to 1945. The CCKW designation comes from GMC factory codes designation key features of the truck: **C** – designed in 1941; **C** – conventional cab; **K** – all-wheel drive; **W** – dual rear wheels The bulldozer was creating paths across the terraces for vehicles with supplies, tanks and Marine rifle companies to move inland as well as make protective revetments for ammunition dumps, fuel storage and medical aid stations. Landing craft and a destroyer warship are in the background. (Photo: *Pfc R.R. Dodds*) (*NARA*)

(**Opposite, above**) Two 4th Division Marines examine two demolished LVTs from Japanese bi-horned landmines, used as anti-boat obstacles and enemy artillery. These landmines weighed 110lb and contained 46lb of explosive (60 per cent Tri-Nitro-Toluene, 40 per cent Tetra-Nitro-Aniline), were 10 inches high and 20 inches diameter at their base. Two leader horns protruded towards the top to set off the detonation when crushed by an LVT or other amphibious vehicle. (Photo: *SSgt M. Kauffman*) (*NARA*)

(**Opposite, below**) 21st Marines probe for mines with bayonets on an Airfield No. 2 taxiway on 27 February 1945. Two days earlier, the 21st Marines reverted to the 3rd Division after temporary attachment to the 4th Division. The 3rd Division's mission was clearance of the central portion of the Motoyama Plateau via an advance across Airfield No. 2 through Motoyama Village to the unfinished Airfield No. 3. The 21st Marines moved towards a network of Japanese bunkers armed with AT guns aimed straight down the flat, unobstructed north–south runway of Airfield No. 2, which were protected by interlocking pillboxes that laid down curtains of machine-gun fire. In addition to 21st Marines casualties, eight M4A2 medium tanks had moved less than 30 yards onto the airstrip when one triggered a land mine and the tank's treads were blown off. The next M4A2 moved ahead another 10 yards and it was disabled by a buried 500lb aerial bomb. Bunkers from the north end of the runway fired volleys from their 47mm AT guns, destroying the next three M4A2s, causing the surviving three tanks to retreat to the reverse side of a ridge on the west side of the runway. (Photo: *Cpl R.R. Robbins*) (*NARA*)

A Marine bomb disposal company collects various Japanese aerial bombs, which when buried with a detonation device, functioned as landmines (called 'aerial torpedoes') that could destroy or disable oncoming Marine tanks. (Photo: *TSgt G.B. Kress*) (*NARA*)

Since Iwo Jima was almost devoid of fresh water, a 21st Marine, 3rd Division unloads 5-gallon cans full of purified water from an M29 Weasel, which early on were dispersed at diverse island sites by ships using onboard evaporators to generate the water for container filling. After beachheads were secured, desalination stations were constructed to generate more purified water. Desalination devices could generate 250 gallons of potable water each hour. By 23 February, the Japanese were placed on a severe water ration as Japanese officers and men suffered from lack of water, gathering rainwater in empty barrels. (Photo: *TSgt J.A. Mundell*) *(NARA)*

A 5th Division M1917A 0.50-inch calibre Browning water-cooled MG crew fires in support of 28th Marines advancing on Mount Suribachi on 21 February. A labelled water can and the expended shell casings and open ammunition boxes attest to the heavy supporting fire that this Marine MG crew provided. (Photo: *Sgt L.R. Burmeister*) *(NARA)*

(**Opposite, above**) Marine 2nd Separate Engineer Battalion and the 62nd Naval Construction Battalion (CB) ('Seabees') scrape and roll a captured Airfield No. 1 runway, with Mount Suribachi in the background. The 133rd Naval Construction Battalion was to repair the captured Airfield No. 1, but it incurred so many casualties supporting Colonel Wensinger's 23rd Marines, 4th Division, that the assignment was ultimately given to the 62nd Naval Construction Battalion to get the airfield operational. (*NARA*)

(**Opposite, below**) 5th Division troops continue their inland assault towards the south side of Airfield No. 1 at 0900 hours on 20 February. Crossing open terrain, two Marines take cover in a shell hole, with the one crouching holding an M1 semi-automatic 0.30-inch calibre carbine rifle. The upright Marine carries a Model 1912 Winchester 12-gauge pump shotgun, which was utilized in the PTO by Marines against the Japanese in close combat. Deadly, reliable and compact, it was perfectly suited to clear Japanese trenches, bunkers and positions once inside them. (Photo: *WO O. Newcomb*) (*NARA*)

(**Above**) Two Marines haul the tow bar of an M3A4 Utility hand cart on 24 February across a furrowed section of Iwo Jima's terrain towards the front lines with scrubwood visible (left) and Mount Suribachi looming (background). 'Carts, Hand, M3 and M3A4 (Utility)', 'Carts M4 and M4A1 (0.30-inch calibre MG)', 'Carts M5 and M5A1 (0.50-inch calibre MG)' and 'Carts M6 and M6A1 (81mm mortar)' were all developed in the 1930s. Marines stowed kit items and personal weapons, flamethrowers with the necessary fuel and nitrogen cylinders, as well as disassembled mortars for manhandled transport. (Photo: *Cpl J. Schwartz*) (*NARA*)

(**Above**) A Marine rifleman quickly advances past a recently killed Japanese soldier less than 50 yards from the front lines, with enemy bullets hitting the remaining tree branches, on 3 March. Marine misconceptions about Japanese marksmanship were quickly dispelled as enemy action shifted from larger-calibre artillery and mortars to small infantry unit, close-range fighting where terrain features mitigated use of Marine artillery and tanks. (Photo: *TSgt B. Ferneyhough*) (*NARA*)

(**Opposite, above**) Sulphur holes emit foul-smelling fumes amid shell craters, giving Iwo Jima its moniker 'Sulphur Island'. When the Japanese dug their maze of 11 miles of tunnels connecting underground barracks, hospitals, ammunition dumps, water supplies and foodstuffs, they wore gas masks to suppress the nauseating smell of sulphur. (Photo: *Sgt A.J. Kiely, Jr.*) (*NARA*)

(**Opposite, below**) Two 21st Marines, 3rd Division maintain a vigil against Japanese snipers from a destroyed concrete-lined casemate housing a disabled Japanese 5-inch naval gun while experiencing the sulphur fumes emanating from the ground. Marines often warmed coffee at sulphur pits. (*NARA*)

(**Opposite, above**) Ammunition is unloaded in 'chain gang' style by Marines aboard an LCVP, tossing tubes filled with individual rounds to others ashore for stacking onto dry matting, on 21 February, just before an air raid siren sounded. Rough surf conditions, evidenced by wrecked assault vessels (left background), prevented any unloading from larger vessels. (Photo: *Cpl E. Jones*) *(NARA)*

(**Opposite, below**) Marines in the 3rd Division sector's congested beachhead unload artillery ammunition from an LVT 2 amphibious tractor, which was an improvement over the LVT 1 as it used the engine and transmission of the M3 Light Tank. In later versions, the engine was moved from the rear, which restricted cargo space, to the front. The LVT 2 had a crew of three, and had 12mm of armour along with a 0.5-inch calibre MG and two 0.3-inch calibre MGs. On land, an LVT 2 had a speed of 17mph, with a maximum water speed of 6mph. (Photo: *Sgt K.W. Altfather*) *(NARA)*

(**Above**) A Marine shore party unloads artillery ammunition from a GMC DUKW into a hastily excavated beach ammunition pit. The unarmoured DUKW, carrying no defensive armament, debuted in 1942. The acronym for this amphibious truck was: **D** – GM's code for 1942; **U** – utility amphibious; **K** – all-wheel drive ability; **W** – twin rear axles. The DUKW, derived from the GMC 6 × 6 truck, had a boat-shaped hull for buoyancy and carried supplies from ships to the beach. They could also travel inland and were capable of carrying troops and light artillery, such as 75mm pack or 105mm howitzers. Another variant could fire rockets and carry mortars. Over 21,000 of these vehicles were built and although reliable and sturdy, fared poorly in rough seas and surf, often taking on water. It had a maximum land speed of 50mph and a maximum water speed of 6mph. (Photo: *SSgt M.A. Cornelius*) *(NARA)*

(**Opposite, above**) 12th Marines, 3rd Division unload 75mm artillery ammunition from an International Harvester M2 1-ton 4 × 4 truck (M-2-4 4 × 4) near the shore at an impromptu ammunition dump. Tyre chains were helpful on the island's difficult terrain and soft volcanic sand. These trucks were transformed into offensive vehicles with the addition of racks for M8 4.5-inch HE barrage rockets. (Photo: *Sgt H.W. Rohland*) (*NARA*)

(**Opposite, below**) 3rd Division Marines unload 81mm mortar rounds from an M29 Weasel-drawn trailer. The tracked Weasel hauled supplies to forward positions, carried wounded Marines and strung communication wire, among other tasks. The M29 was made by Studebaker on an original design by British inventor Geoffrey Pyke for operations in snow to attack Nazi forces and heavy water plants in Norway; however, the Norwegian mission was cancelled. About 15,000 were made and were invaluable in hauling loads over muddy and sandy terrain that wheeled vehicles could not traverse. Due to PTO surf conditions, the M29C or Water Weasel, which had fore and aft buoyancy cells and twin rudders, was operationally limited to inland waterways as in the ETO. In heavily mined zones, the M29 was able to cross as its ground pressure was often too low to detonate AT mines. (Photo: *Sgt R.R. Robbins*) (*NARA*)

(**Above**) Two Marines sit in a quarter-ton, four-wheel-drive jeep, produced by Willys-Overland, Bantam or Ford, the latter calling their model the Ford GP (for general purpose), hence its moniker. A solitary Marine holding his M1 semi-automatic 0.3-inch calibre carbine is situated atop a trailer loaded with ammunition for the front lines. The jeep had a maximum highway speed of 50mph and could carry five soldiers or 800lb of cargo, and when fully loaded was able to go 20 miles on a single gallon of gasoline. The jeep also hauled medical supplies, rations and communication gear, and could tow small artillery pieces. An estimated 650,000 jeeps (standard and modified) were produced by the war's end in 1945, with the majority built by Willys-Overland in Toledo, Ohio. (Photo: *Cpl E. Jones*) (*NARA*)

Marine Rocket Reconnaissance trucks, modifications of International Harvester M2 1-ton 4×4 trucks (M-2-4 4×4), fire their M8 4.5-inch HE barrage rockets before these provisional rocket detachments attached to Marine assault divisions quickly departed to avoid Japanese counterbattery fire. The rocket launching system comprised three box-shaped launchers with each containing a dozen 4.5-inch rockets. A good crew could launch the three dozen rockets within a few seconds from their truck, modified to carry the ordnance with a reinforced tailgate as a blast shield and a hydraulic jack to raise the individual rocket launchers. After a blanket of HE ordnance landed on enemy targets, Japanese artillery and mortars delivered heavy return fire after enemy spotters acquired aiming from the smoke and dust emanating from the fired rockets. On Iwo, the 1st Provisional Rocket Detachment supported the 4th Marine Division, while the 3rd Provisional Rocket Detachment supported the 5th Marine Division. The 3rd Marine Division did not have such a unit during the campaign. The two Provisional Rocket Detachments fired more than 30,000 rockets to support the two Marine divisions. In northern Iwo Jima, the rockets' short range, angle of fire, and a barrage of thirty-six fired produced a saturation effect on enemy targets. (Photo: *SSgt R.R. Robbins*) (*NARA*)

A tank dozer clears a path through a rocky depression while Marines wait to the side for the armoured vehicle's blade to pass, on 9 March, during northern Iwo Jima fighting amid ridges, crevices and ravines. Tanks were of little assistance in this terrain unless existing trails or new routes were carved out of the rock by the tank dozers and armoured bulldozers. Even then, the trails were mined and covered by AT guns, and the construction of approaches was time-consuming and costly, as exemplified in the 23rd Marines, 4th Division sector of action, where the Japanese fiercely resisted from Hill 382 on 25 February, repelling attack after attack by the Marines from the west. A tank dozer and Marine engineers laboured most of that day to clear a route forward for the M4A3 tanks of Company B, 4th TB to move forward to support the infantry. (Photo: *Sgt J.T. Dreyfuss*) (*NARA*)

A Marine M3 37mm AT gun crew hauls their cannon up a rock-strewn road on 24 February. Antiquated as an AA gun, it was deployed as an AT weapon against lightly armoured Japanese tanks. The gun's light weight did not require vehicular towing if urgently needed and was effective against pillboxes and MG nests. When firing fragmentation ammunition it served as a 'giant shotgun' against massed Japanese infantry attacks. Terrain such as above was traversed by the 4th Division moving towards 'The Amphitheatre', a semi-circular rise of ground to the south-east of 'Charlie-Dog Ridge', (the latter named after its designated map grid square coordinates) on 1 March. Combined use of 105mm howitzers of the 14th Marines (Artillery), 81mm and 60mm mortar fire from 4th Division platoons and companies, MGs, and a 37mm AT gun neutralized a number of enemy positions on 'Charlie-Dog Ridge'. (Photo: *Sgt J.T. Dreyfuss*) (*NARA*)

Two 4th Division officers stand at the 'Amphitheatre', a bowl-shaped depression with massive boulders concealing a honeycomb of defensive positions, which became an infamous combat locale for the 4th Division, looking south-west towards Mount Suribachi in the haze (far background). The 4th Division had to cross this relatively flat and open ground to reach the strong enemy positions in this area. On the three terraces comprising the 'Amphitheatre', the Japanese had built concrete blockhouses along the south side of the depression. These were linked by 700 yards of tunnels with walls lined with communications and electric light cables. AT guns and MGs covered all approaches from the south. Other heavily contested locales for the 4th Division in this vicinity included Hill 382, situated east of Airfield No. 2 and north-west of the ruins of Minami Village, one of five of Iwo Jima's villages. Due west of Minami Village was a craggy elevation called 'Turkey Knob', which had a large communications centre made of reinforced concrete. From 'Turkey Knob's' top, all of southern Iwo Jima was visible. This entire sector became known as the 'Meatgrinder', to the 4th Division. Each of these positions contained vast underground networks to other parts of the island and provided cover for the enemy from the immense Marine and USN bombardment. It would take the 4th Division seven horrendous days and innumerable casualties to reduce the 'Meatgrinder' entirely. (Photo: *SSgt M. Kauffman*) (*NARA*)

(**Above**) Five Marines of the 1st Battalion, 24th Marines (regimental CO Colonel Walter I. Jordan), 4th Division move to assault 'The Quarry' by climbing up a steep, rocky slope on 19 February. The Marine (foreground) holds his folded M1A1 bazooka, which was a metal barrel open at both ends that was used to fire an electrically ignited rocket projectile with a shaped 2.36-inch charge warhead, enabling the infantryman to successfully reduce, at some distance, fortified pillboxes and bunkers. This photograph was taken on D-Day after a hellacious attack on this height was made by the 25th Marines, 4th Division (CO Colonel John R. Lanigan). By 1745 hours, the 2nd Battalion, 25th Marines gained the high ground and Company L, 3rd Battalion, 25th Marines reached the top of 'The Quarry' by 1830 hours. Contact between the 2nd and 3rd Battalions, 25th Marines was lost during the attack but was re-established by 1900 hours. Company B, 1st Battalion, 24th Marines proceeded to relieve Company L, 3rd Battalion, 25th Marines in its position atop 'The Quarry', held by only a handful of Marines during the evening. Lieutenant

Colonel Justice M. Chambers, CO 3rd Battalion, 25th Marines' frontline strength was down to 150 Marines as his battalion lost more than half its officers and nearly 25 per cent of its enlisted strength on that day. Capture of the key high ground was essential to the success of the D-Day assault as it anchored the right flank of the VAC positions. Chambers was awarded a Congressional Medal of Honor for his 'fearless disregard for his own life and leading his depleted battalion by example'. On 23 February, while directing the Marines' first rocket barrage, Lieutenant Colonel Chambers was wounded by enemy machine-gun fire and required evacuation and medical retirement. (Photo: *Pfc J.B. Cochran*) *(NARA)*

(**Below**) Three 9th Marines, 3rd Division – one on either side of the large rock and one atop the ridge, far right – use HE charges to blast Japanese occupants in a quarrylike ravine in northern Iwo Jima. In this rugged terrain, the Japanese strengthened the natural defences by digging and building, changing the entire landscape into a fortress. MG positions controlled draws, while mortars delivered fire on routes of approach, including the crests, forward, and reverse slopes of ridges. (Photo: *TSgt G.B. Kress*) *(NARA)*

(**Above**) A Japanese Type 97 Chi-Ha medium tank, with a short-barrelled 57mm turret gun, is revetted in a rocky enclosure in a 21st Marines, 3rd Division sector, and has been disabled by USN bombardment. The Chi-Ha had a crew of four, and 25mm armour on the gun mantlet. The 57mm turret gun was a carry-over from the Type 89 I-Go medium tank. It had a low silhouette in comparison to other IJA tanks of that time. In 1942, a new version of the Chi-Ha was produced with a larger, three-man turret and a high-velocity 47mm turret gun, and was called the 'Type 97 medium Chi-Ha tank variant, the Shinhōtō Chi-Ha'. (Photo: *Cpl F.E. DeOme*) (*NARA*)

(**Opposite**) A revetted Type 97 Chi-Ha medium tank of Baron Nishi's 26th Tank Regiment is shown with a short-barrelled 57mm turret gun sighted on the approaches to Airfield No. 2, with a Marine inspecting for snipers. The terrain dictated tactics and IJA tanks were emplaced in hull defilade positions or even buried up to their turrets. On 28 February, the 21st Marines, 3rd Division, after relieving the battered 9th Marines, were confronted by some of the few remaining Japanese tanks, which were wiped out by bazookas and aerial sorties, leaving only three operational. (Photo: *SSgt M. Kauffman*) (*NARA*)

(**Above**) A Japanese Type 97 medium Chi-Ha tank variant. This Shinhōtō Chi-Ha is positioned between two earth banks to create a fortified position. This tank had a high-velocity 47mm gun in a newly designed turret, which was an improvement over the Type 97 Chi-Ha's short-barrelled 57mm gun, intended primarily for infantry support. The 47mm gun could penetrate the sides and rear of the Marine M4 medium tank, contributing to its reputation as the best Japanese tank in the PTO. Hill 382 bristled with field pieces, AT guns and some 47mm and 57mm tank guns in revetted positions. (*NARA*)

(**Opposite, above**) Only the turret of a hull down, camouflaged Japanese Type 97 Chi-Ha medium tank with its Type 1 47mm gun is visible for Marines' inspection in northern Iwo Jima. The tank's thin armour only protected against hand-held weapons and was an easy target for Marine AT guns and tanks, hence its revetted position with only the turret exposed. When mobile, these tanks provided infantry support and were deployed in small groups on the numerous Japanese-occupied islands in the PTO. (*NARA*)

(**Opposite, below**) A 4th Division Marine, with his M1 0.30-inch calibre semi-automatic carbine rifle, kneels beside the motor portion of a Type 98 Japanese 320mm Spigot mortar (nicknamed 'Ghost Rocket') and its baseplate within a concrete reinforced emplacement with other parts (right). These enormous weapons were operated by the IJA 20th Independent Artillery Mortar Battalion. The mortar tube rested on a steel baseplate that, in turn, was supported by a wooden platform. The mortarmen had to manually shove and push the base platform to change the shell's deflection. Due to their weight, these mortars remained fixed during battle, with their gun crews living in caves housing the ordnance. The Japanese had twelve of these 320mm mortars. (Photo: *Sgt A.R. Morejohn*) (*NARA*)

(**Above**) The various parts of the Type 98 320mm Spigot mortar lying on the ground are shown (left to right): the head (or nose), body, and motor with another motor portion standing (far left). The head was packed with a fuse and explosives. The motor carried the propellant charge. Unlike a conventional mortar, the 5-foot-long, 23-inch-wide finned, projectile-packed 675lb HE was fitted around the top of the 31.7-inch-long mortar tube, which was only 10 inches wide, instead of being dropped down the barrel, making the mortar a spigot type. For firing, the finned shell could be hurled to a maximum of almost 1,500 yards, depending on the powder charge. Different-sized powder charges altered the shot's range. The barrels could only handle five or six shots before becoming unusable. Along with the 8-inch IJN rocket, the Spigot mortar instilled terror among Marines due to the projectile's inaccuracy creating uncertainty as to where it would explode. Relatively few Marine casualties were incurred by this weapon due to minimal fragmentation. (Photo: *Sgt A.R. Morejohn*) (*NARA*)

(**Opposite**) A captured Japanese Type 10 120mm DP (AA and CD) naval gun is situated on a pedestal mount in a camouflaged position reinforced with sand-filled fuel drums. This gun was secondary armament on a number of IJN aircraft carriers and cruisers and the main armament on smaller ships. The gun's barrel length was 18 feet and it fired Fixed QF 120mm HE or incendiary shrapnel shells at a rate of ten to twelve rounds per minute. In a horizontal position for coastal defence, it had an effective firing range of 17,000 yards, and in a vertical AA position, its effective firing range was 27,900 feet. (*NARA*)

6466

(**Opposite, above**) A group of 28th Marines, 5th Division with a captured Japanese Rising Sun good-luck flag (*Yosegaki Hinomaru*) sit atop the barrel of a demolished Japanese 120mm/45 3rd Year Type naval CD gun in a wrecked concrete casemate with a destroyed enemy MG atop it at Mount Suribachi's base, on 23 February. The small Japanese national flag was inscribed with short messages wishing victory, safety and good luck by friends and family of Japanese servicemen to carry as mementos from home. After the war, many such flags came back with American soldiers as souvenirs. *Hinomaru*, the design for the captured flag, translates literally as 'circle of the sun', initially adopted under Emperor Meiji's reign in 1870, and continues to be Japan's national flag. (Photo: *SSgt M.A. Cornelius*) (*NARA*)

(**Opposite, below**) A Marine sentry armed with a 0.30-inch calibre M1 carbine rifle stands guard over a destroyed Japanese 120mm/45 3rd Year Type naval CD gun in its destroyed casemate at the foot of Mount Suribachi. Concealed casemated artillery caused innumerable Marine casualties at the beachhead and destroyed scores of assault craft transporting them to shore at the invasion's start. In the IJN, this naval CD gun was also used on destroyers and torpedo boats. (*NARA*)

(**Above**) A disabled Japanese 12.7cm/40 (5-inch) Type 88 (submarine) or 89 (warship) naval gun in its concrete and rock open casemate in the 21st Marines, 3rd Division sector. Mount Suribachi is in the far background, while Marine vehicles, tents and equipment are present. These ship guns were present in casemates throughout the PTO and could fire eight to fourteen rounds per minute, which explains the wall of artillery fire that rained down on the Marine beachheads on 19 February. (Photo: *Cpl F.E. DeOme*) (*NARA*)

(**Opposite, above**) A Japanese Type 88 75mm pedestal-mounted AA gun in an open concrete-rimmed position was destroyed by direct USN bombardment. The barrel length was 10 feet with a crew of twelve servicing the weapon, which fired a 75mm shell with semi-automatic loading and firing of up to fifteen to twenty rounds per minute. This AA gun was an effective AT gun when firing AP shells horizontally, explaining the high number of Marine tanks and amphibious tractors disabled on or near the beachhead and inland, especially at Airfield No. 2. Its maximal vertical range of 23,790 feet made it ineffective against B-29 Superfortresses flying at 31,860. (Photo: *Sgt N. Ragus*) (*NARA*)

(**Opposite, below**) A captured camouflaged Japanese Type 1 47mm high muzzle velocity AT gun revetted in an earthen dugout. Firing AP shells, this gun could pierce the side armour of an M4A2 or M4A3 tank at 800 yards. It was breech-loaded with a split trail, and replaced the Type 94 37mm AT gun. The Japanese had five independent AT gun battalions also deployed in FA roles on Iwo Jima. (*NARA*)

(**Above**) A covered, reinforced position houses a Type 38 75mm field gun with characteristic large wheels and gun shield in the 4th Division sector. The Type 38 designation reflected the thirty-eighth year of Emperor Meiji's reign (1905). It was based on a 1905 German design purchased by Japan, and fired a Fixed QF 75mm shell with an effective range of 9,000 yards and a firing rate of ten to twelve rounds per minute. Despite its obsolescence, this gun served in many PTO battles. (Photo: *V.W. Branch*) (*NARA*).

(**Above**) A Japanese short-barrelled Type 38 75mm field gun captured by the 28th Marines, 5th Division in a rocky crevice on Hill 362-A, on 3 March. This gun fired HE, AP, shrapnel, incendiary, smoke, illumination and gas shells. On 2 March, Lieutenant Colonel Chandler Johnson, CO 2nd Battalion 28th Marines, who ordered the attack on Mount Suribachi on 23 February, was killed by an HE shell as his Marines reduced enemy positions, so by nightfall, Hill 362-A was reasonably secured. Hill 362-A was heavily fortified, serving as the western anchor of the Japanese cross-island defences, giving the enemy an unobstructed view over the entire south-western half of the island and most of the Motoyama Plateau. Before the 5th Division assault began on 27 February, this terrain feature received a naval bombardment, a 4.5-inch rocket truck barrage, and USN carrier plane attack. (Photo: *Sgt J.T. Dreyfuss*) (*NARA*)

(**Opposite, above**) A twin mount Type 96 25mm AT/AA gun is emplaced in a ground-level fortified position near one of the two airfields. An entrance to a personnel shelter and ammunition storage area is present (right). This automatic cannon, built on a variant of the French Hotchkiss 25mm AA gun except that it was designed by the Japanese as a DP weapon against armoured vehicles and aircraft, sits on fixed low pedestal mounts. There were also single- and triple-barrel guns produced. It had a 110-rounds-per-minute effective rate of fire with a 15-round box magazine, but firing ceased every time the hand-loaded magazines had to be changed. This weapon was most effective when used at 1,100 yards or less. (Photo: *SSgt M. Kauffman*) (*NARA*)

(**Below**) A Marine examines a Japanese 200mm (8-inch) wooden rocket launcher, which was captured in March and fired 8-inch rockets with motors from the wooden chute. Accurate fire was almost impossible, but the huge shells, with a range of over 2,100 yards, made a disquieting rumbling noise hurtling through the air. Hitting the Marine beach-head on 19 February, the rocket's detonation left a wide area of destruction. Kuribayashi had been given seventy of these rocket launchers, with fifty rounds for each one. (*NARA*)

A Type 97 150mm mortar, designated as a 'high-angle infantry gun', captured by the 28th Marines, 5th Division near Mount Suribachi in late February. This was one of the largest enemy mortars used next to the 320mm Spigot mortar and it was almost twice the size of the largest American 81mm mortar. The Type 97 150mm mortar weighed over 700lb and required a crew of ten men to fire the 57lb HE shell a maximum of 2,187 yards. This weapon was used to almost constantly bombard the Marine lines during the early days after the 19 February amphibious assault. (Photo: *SSgt M. Kauffman*) (*NARA*)

A captured Japanese Type 97 81mm infantry mortar was a smooth-bore, muzzle-loading weapon manufactured in 1942 in the Osaka Army Arsenal. This weapon broke down into three sections for transport. It weighed 145lb and fired HE shells from 0.75–1.9 miles depending on the round's weight. (*NARA*)

(**Above**) A 4th Division Marine stands near the rear of a Type 4 200mm (8-inch) mobile rocket launcher mounted on a two-wheeled steel carriage for mobility. It sits in a heavily camouflaged, concrete-reinforced emplacement as the Marine holds the launcher's crude elevating mechanism that maximally raised the stovepipe-like barrel to 75 degrees. For traverse movement, the trail had to be moved. This breech-loaded weapon's main disadvantage was overheating after two or three rounds, requiring sixty minutes' cooling before resuming firing. The weapon used a modified IJN spin-stabilised 8-inch rocket weighing about 200lb, with a range of 2,000 yards. (Photo: *SSgt M. Kauffman*) (*NARA*)

(**Opposite, above**) A group of Japanese single-horned, conical-shaped JLXVI mines removed from landing beaches by Marine engineers is cordoned off. These beach and inland AT mines were 12 inches high and 14 inches at their base, with one carrying handle on each side of a black steel case. They were buried with only their single lead horn (pile of unattached ones, far right) protruding above the ground. When the horn was crushed, a vial of acid in the truncated cone broke and ran into a battery cup producing an electrical circuit made by wires leading to a detonator to set off the main charge. Some were found in groups of three with the horns lashed to a length of bar to increase the danger area. Weighing 72lb and containing 22lb of Type 98 explosive (60 per cent Tri-Nitro-Toluene, 40 per cent Tetra-Nitro-Aniline), these mines could disable a medium tank. There were also larger and more powerful bi-horned, hemisphere-shaped JLXIII anti-boat mines. (Photo: *SSgt M. Kauffman*) (*NARA*)

(**Below**) A Marine aims an SMG at an opening of a Japanese pillbox three hours after the initial landing on 19 February. This fortified position was part of a network of concealed emplacements for artillery, mortars and MGs that covered the landing zones with interlocking fields of fire. Eliminating Japanese pillboxes and underground emplacements was slow and costly as Marines deployed flamethrowers, satchel charges, grenades and personal weapons. Many of the pillboxes were log and concrete reinforced, especially protecting the airfields. A Marine flamethrower, Congressional Medal of Honor winner Corporal Hershel Williams, discovered that once you got behind the pillboxes, the Marines gained the advantage. (*NARA*)

(**Opposite, above**) A Marine private examines a volcanic sand- and rock-fortified Japanese pillbox, which was knocked out on 24 February and housed a Type 90 75mm artillery piece used in an AT role. Many of these pillboxes were demolished by naval and aerial bombardment; however, after the landing, Marine flamethrowers, demolition teams and tanks were required for neutralizing those enemy positions still operational. Many of the bunkers were almost impossible to spot until the defenders opened fire. (Photo: *Sgt D.G. Christian*) (*NARA*)

(**Opposite, below**) A Marine with his M1 Garand 30.06 calibre semi-automatic rifle with attached bayonet waits for a flamethrower at the opening of a Japanese log- and rock-fortified cave carved into a hummock, on 3 March. Some of northern Iwo Jima's most formidable defences were in crevices and caves, patches of scrubwood and rocky cliffs, which constituted unassuming terrain that formed the backbone of Kuribayashi's positions. The heavily reinforced positions ranged from one-man rifle pits and sandbagged caves to blockhouses with reinforced concrete walls. (Photo: *Sgt J.T. Dreyfuss*) (*NARA*)

(**Above**) A 5th Division Marine artillery spotter uses a pair of high-powered IJN ship binoculars to view Japanese positions on Mount Suribachi's slope on 22 February. Captured enemy equipment and positions were frequently utilized during the Marines' advance. (Photo: *Pvt G. Burns*) (*YANK magazine / USAHEC*)

(**Above**) A Marine patrol, including a heavily kitted Marine carrying an ammunition box and a flamethrower, cautiously moves along a rock and scrubwood-strewn trail over a ridge on the front lines of northern Iwo Jima on 27 February. During this stage of the combat, burning out caves while crawling through the rocky wasteland of Kuribayashi's defences was commonplace in the VAC northern drive. (Photo: *Sgt J.T. Dreyfuss*) (*NARA*)

(**Opposite, above**) Two 28th Marines, 5th Division, Private Richard Klatt and Private 1st Class Wilfred Voegeli, use flamethrowers on Mount Suribachi defences on 23 February, with dense scrubwood as a terrain feature. This thick brush at the volcano's base hid an extensive network of trenches, AT ditches and camouflaged pillboxes as many of the latter were sand-covered, giving them the appearance of mounds. After the pillboxes were reduced by the flamethrowers and the ammunition exploding inside them had ceased, Marines of the 5th Engineer Battalion sealed them with demolitions to prevent Japanese reoccupation. (Photo: *Pvt R. Campbell*) (*NARA*)

(**Opposite, below**) A Marine flamethrower, backed by three riflemen, applies a jet of fuel to Japanese troops lurking in a rocky crevice on northern Iwo Jima on 6 March. The portable M2-2 flamethrower, with the three full tanks (two each with 2 gallons of napalm-thickened fuel and a smaller third one with pressurized nitrogen as propellant) weighed 68lb and had a new cartridge-based ignition system in a revolver type magazine (flamethrower's left hand), with a total of five possible ignitions before reloading, making it much more reliable than the earlier M1 and M1A1 models, which used a spark plug to ignite the fuel as it was projected at the target. The maximum range of the M2-2 was 80 yards, with the duration of each ignition maintained for no more than ten seconds. (Photo: *Sgt L.R. Burmeister*) (*NARA*)

(**Above**) A Marine M4A3 tank equipped with the USN Mk I flamethrower, deemed to be one of the most valuable weapons employed fighting the entrenched Japanese on Iwo Jima, fires a jet of fuel at an enemy position. While the landing force relied on portable backpack M2-2 flamethrowers to combat the innumerable enemy fortifications, combining the technology of directed flame from armoured vehicles was optimally achieved. In the Marianas campaign, the Marines modified M3A1 light tanks with the Canadian Ronson flame system, but the small vehicles were vulnerable to low-calibre Japanese guns. At Peleliu, the 1st Marine Division mounted an improvised Mk I system on a minimally armoured LVT-4, which limited the system's effectiveness. The first modification of the M4A3 tank for the Iwo Jima battle involved the installation of the small E4-5 mechanized flamethrower in the bow MG position. However, short range, limited fuel supply and difficult aiming were problems. A better flamethrower design resulted from collaboration between the US Army Chemical Warfare Service at Schofield Barracks on Oahu and Fleet Marine Tankers in Hawaii before the invasion. The improved modification positioned the Mk I flamethrower within the M4A3 turret, replacing the 75mm main turret gun with a similarly appearing launch tube. The modified system could be aimed like a conventional turret gun that could spew napalm-thickened fuel 150 yards for a duration of just over one minute. The Marines dubbed these armoured vehicles 'Zippo

Tanks' after the cigarette lighter. However, only eight M4A3 tanks with the Mk I flame-thrower were produced in time for the Iwo Jima campaign, with four going to the 5th TB and the other four to the 4th TB. Northern Iwo's rough terrain and Japanese gunfire took their toll on the eight 'Zippo Tanks' but Marine maintenance crews ceaselessly worked to maintain their operational status. (Photo: *SSgt M. Kauffman*) (NARA)

(**Below**) Marine Corporal Elmo Casado, 5th Engineer Battalion, prepares a demolition charge of HE to destroy an enemy fortified position at Mount Suribachi's base on 23 February in order to prevent it from being reoccupied by the Japanese. The demolition charge was often attached to a pole to insert the HE pack into the aperture of a Japanese pillbox and enable the Marine engineer to take cover from the exploding debris after its detonation. (Photo: *Pvt G. Burns*) (YANK *magazine* / USAHEC)

(**Above**) Two Marines crouch behind a rock wall while a third (foreground) bends near an adjacent stone structure after an HE charge detonates on a Japanese fortified position. A bazooka leans against the rock wall (background), which killed the Japanese occupants before sealing the enemy position with the HE. (*NARA*)

(**Opposite, above**) A Marine from an engineer battalion lies close to the ground as his HE demolition charge detonates to destroy a Japanese pillbox and send debris flying skywards. The image demonstrates the proximity that Marine engineers worked with to detonate the HE. (*NARA*)

(**Opposite, below**) 4th Division Marines hover by a destroyed Japanese blockhouse just inland from the landing beaches on 19 February. Marines burrowed into shell holes in the volcanic sand while dead combatant bodies lay uncovered (foreground). Scattered kit, equipment, fuel cans, and a conical-shaped, single-horn Japanese AT landmine (left foreground) litter the battlefield. (Photo: *Associated Press photographer Joe Rosenthal*) (*NARA*)

(**Above**) Marines shelter in a previously occupied Japanese concrete-walled blockhouse that housed a Type 1 47mm AT gun with a bullet-riddled gun shield (left background). The enemy blockhouse functioned as a Marine CP 30 yards from the front lines. The height of the blockhouse was limited since the 47mm AT gun had a very low profile and the IJA gunners operated from a kneeling or prone position with a gun shield for protection. (Photo: *Sgt N. Ragus*) (NARA)

(**Opposite, above**) Marine observers in a shell crater spot artillery fire during the tank battle at the northern end of Airfield No. 2 on 25 February. Wrecked Japanese aircraft provided some cover for the Marine OP. Two taxiways led from the north-western tip of Airfield No. 1 to the second airfield. The original plan was for tanks from the 5th TB, followed by those of the 3rd TB, to gain access to Airfield No. 2 by proceeding along the western taxiway, while armour from the 4th TB used the eastern taxiway. However, 5th TB M4A3s along the western route ran into mines and Japanese AT fire. Five tanks were quickly disabled as the remaining tanks fought back to the bivouac area, and the western approach was abandoned. Now all tanks would have to use the eastern taxiway in the VAC movement to Airfield No. 2. The 3rd Division two regiments were responsible for clearing the central portion of the Motoyama Plateau encompassing Airfield Nos. 2 and 3 and Motoyama Village. The 3rd Division became engaged in furious combat at Hill 199 OBOE at the northern edge of Airfield No. 2. The designations 199 OBOE and PETER were derived from target grid locations on the island map and not from elevations. These hills were actually about 360 feet high. (Photo: *Sgt R. Cooke*) (NARA)

(**Below**) A Marine with his M1 30.06 calibre semi-automatic Garand rifle (front) and another Marine with a 30.06 M1918A2 BAR inch forward under heavy Japanese gunfire near a captured enemy blockhouse at Airfield No. 2 on 25 February. The M1 Garand had an eight-round stripper clip that could be loaded into the top of the magazine, while the BAR had a twenty-round detachable magazine, both of which being superior to the bolt-action Japanese Arisaka rifles. The BAR was designed to be carried by infantrymen during an assault advance while supported by the sling over the shoulder, or be fired from the hip. The BAR could also be fired from a bipod, making it effectively an LMG. At Airfield No. 2, the Japanese sighted their guns down the runways and flat expanse of the Motoyama Plateau along with well-situated minefields; had their artillery and mortars pre-registered for a Marine assault; and utilized a multitude of MG nests and riflemen hidden in strategic positions. (Photo: *Sgt R. Cooke*) *(NARA)*

(**Opposite, above**) Two Marines shelter in a former Japanese sniper position made from three enemy aircraft wings at Airfield No. 2 on 23 February. Mount Suribachi is to the south amid haze (far background) and the airfield's runway is immediately behind the shelter position. More than 800 pillboxes ringed the airfield, mostly on the high ground to the north, and the artillery fired straight down the runways. 'Charlie-Dog Ridge' (named after map coordinates) was a strongly defended area running along the south-eastern edge of the east–west runway on Airfield No. 2. It was secured by the 2nd and 3rd Battalions, 24th Marines, on 24 February. (Photo: *Sgt R. Cooke*) (*NARA*)

(**Opposite, below**) Corporal Leo Bridal, a 5th Division radioman, sits in a Japanese fortified position (note Japanese writing on wall placard at left) at Mount Suribachi's base, which was isolated and captured on 22 February. He uses an EE-8 series field telephone to coordinate Marine artillery fire support during the 28th Marines assault on the volcano. The EE-8 used a wired line with a maximal transmission distance of 7 miles, with D cell batteries to power the signal through the wire to the other phone. A hand crank generated the charge to ring the phone at the other end. (Photo: *Pvt G. Burns*) (YANK *magazine* / USAHEC)

(**Above**) Two Marine signalmen string telephone wire, which was crucial for field telephone communications, across a former Japanese dugout in some thick, dense scrubwood brush on 24 February. The Japanese used a system of dugouts, blockhouses and underground tunnels often concealed with scrubwood, which hid surviving Japanese defenders, as encountered by 28th Marines' patrols during Mount Suribachi's ascent on 23 February. (Photo: *Cpl J. Schwartz*) (*NARA*)

(**Above**) Marine riflemen open fire at the opening of a cave dug out from a rocky ridge covered with sparse vegetation after locating Japanese snipers. Marines were often astonished upon finding livestock and chickens, vegetable gardens, medical supplies and stockpiles of ammunition within multi-level caves. Also, American weapons, grenades, ponchos, shelter halves and leggings were found, taken after Japanese night infiltration of Marine positions or from dead Marines in the field. (*NARA*)

(**Opposite, above**) Hill 382, from the ground looked barren and harmless. However, its sloping summit was a massive OP equipped with high-powered binoculars and elec-tronic artillery-detection that covered the island's entire southern end. Excavated within the hill was a 30 by 40-foot communications centre, with concrete walls 4 feet thick and a steel-reinforced roof able to withstand heavy naval bombardment and direct hits from USN carrier planes' 500lb bombs without serious damage. Across the top of the hill was a destroyed Japanese radar tower, which lay amid a cinder-block building that was a two-storey concrete blockhouse containing artillery and AT weapons. This strongpoint had a ring of camouflaged MGs and steel-covered dugouts for the numerous Japanese snipers that provided mutually supporting fields of fire. (Photo: *Pvt R. Campbell*) (*NARA*)

(**Opposite, below**) A cave on Hill 382, which was the scene of where Sergeant William Genaust, who filmed the second raising of the American flag on Mount Suribachi with his 16mm hand-held moving picture camera, died. He was killed by Japanese grenades after he entered the cave and his body was never found. Kuribayashi had pressed the programme of cave development before the Marines landed. There were many natural caves on the island, and the hills and ridges were excellent for man-made excavations. Cave specialists came from Japan to make measurements and ground tests to draw blueprints for cave fortifications. From experience in China, the Japanese knew that good ventilation, especially with the island's sulphur fumes, could be assured if entrances and exits were built at different levels, and they laid out tunnels within the caves to neutralize blast shocks near the cave mouths. (Photo: *Pvt R. Campbell*) (*NARA*)

A typical Japanese-dug tunnel, which connected the ridge north of Blue Beach 2 near 'The Quarry' in the 4th Division sector to inland enemy defensive positions in the Motoyama district in the north, is shown. The Japanese planned almost 18 miles of underground tunnels. This work commenced in June 1944, but by the time of the Marine landings, only a fraction of the excavation was complete. The ground of Iwo Jima was excellent for tunnelling as the soft volcanic stone could be cut with hand tools. The passages had to be at least 30 feet underground for protection from USN bombardment and Marine heavier artillery once ashore. During the height of the battle, many Marines reported hearing voices and movements coming from below ground. In the north, Kuribayashi's HQ (south of Kitano Point) consisted of a cave system connected by 500 feet of tunnels as much as 75 feet underground. This structure housed the CG's rooms and sections for staff, coding and communications. When Mount Suribachi was isolated, many of the defenders escaped to the north of the island through the maze of tunnels, and in so doing bypassed the Marine lines above ground. (Photo: *Sgt J. Glozak*) (*NARA*)

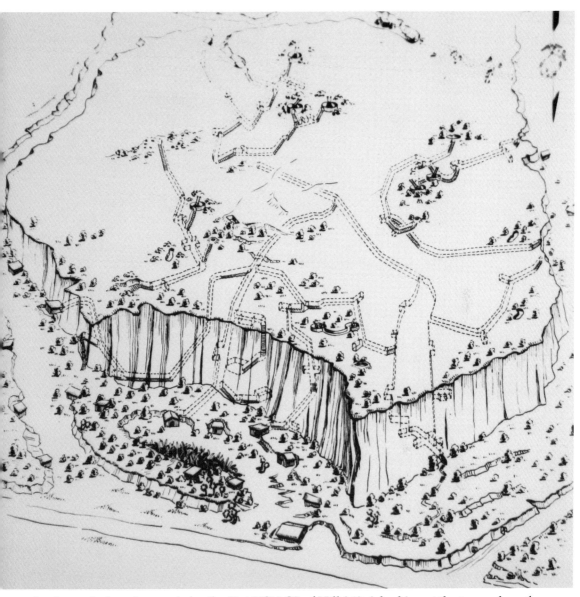

A schematic drawing made by the 31st USN CB of Hill 362-A looking at the top and north face. The dotted lines denote Japanese underground tunnels below the surface of this daunting terrain feature. During the nights, Marines could hear sounds and voices underneath them, as Japanese troops rested or moved in the tunnels below their lines. The Japanese defenders were not on Iwo Jima but in Iwo Jima. A Marine veteran in the 28th Marines, 5th Division, and author, Richard Wheeler, said, 'This was surely one of the strangest battlefields in history, with one side fighting wholly above the ground and the other operating almost wholly within it. ... The strangest thing of all was that the two contestants sometimes made troop movements simultaneously in the same area, one manoeuvring on the surface and the other using tunnels beneath.' *(NARA)*

Four Japanese 8-inch rockets are measured by a 4th Division Marine in a concrete fortified ammunition bunker. (Photo: *SSgt M. Kauffman*) (*NARA*)

Riflemen from 3rd Battalion, 28th Marines, 5th Division storm a northern Iwo Jima ridge in frontal attack in late February. (Photo: *Pfc C. Jones*) (*NARA*)

Chapter Three

Commanders and Combatants

American Commanders

Admiral Raymond A. Spruance, commander US Fifth Fleet, was in overall or operational command of the Iwo Jima campaign. Admiral Chester Nimitz, CINPAC and CINPOA, early on identified the Volcano Islands, situated halfway between the Mariana Islands and Tokyo, as an eventual objective to provide airfields to support a large number of American fighter aircraft to escort heavy bombers attacking Japan from captured and built Mariana Islands airfields. Iwo Jima had two operational and one incomplete airfield.

Admiral Ernest J. King, COMINCH and CNO, in early October 1944 indicated that there were insufficient ground forces in the Pacific to meet the minimum requirements for an invasion of Formosa and the south-east Chinese coast, so his strategic thinking shifted to occupying Iwo Jima in the early winter of 1945, followed by a move to seize Okinawa to sever Japanese air communications throughout the Ryukyu Islands. The JCS accepted King's proposal and immediately issued a new directive on 3 October to occupy Iwo Jima, with a target date of 20 January 1945. On 9 October 1944, Nimitz informed Marine Lieutenant General Holland M. Smith, CG Expeditionary Troops, with his second-in-command, Rear Admiral Harry W. Hill, about the Iwo Jima objective. Smith designated Marine Major General Harry Schmidt as commander of the VAC responsible for planning and executing all Landing Force operations for the 3rd, 4th and 5th Divisions under the respective command of Major General Graves B. Erskine, Major General Clifton B. Cates, and Major General Keller E. Rockey. Vice Admiral Richmond Kelly Turner was the Joint Expeditionary Force Commander of the assault force, initially of 60,000 men combating 23,000 Japanese troops.

By Operation DETACHEMENT's D-Day, 19 February 1945, B-29 attacks against Japan from Saipan, Tinian and Guam had been occurring for three months. USAAF plane and crew losses over Japan and on the long return back to the Mariana bases underscored the need for an intermediate base from which fighters could provide protection over the target and where damaged bombers could land or ditch safely.

VAC planners called for a D-Day landing along a 2-mile stretch of beach between Mount Suribachi and the East Boat Basin along Iwo Jima's south-eastern shore. The 4th and 5th Divisions were to land abreast with the 5th Division on the left. The 3rd Division was to be held as Expeditionary Troops Reserve and when released by VAC it would land over the same beaches on or after D-plus 1. In the

4th Division, the 23rd Marines would land at Yellow 1 and Yellow 2 Beaches. The 24th Marines would land at Blue or Yellow as ordered. The 25th Marines were to land at Blue 1. The 27th Marines, 5th Division would land at Red 1 and Red 2 beaches. The 28th Marines were to land at Green 1, while the 26th Marines were the Corps Reserve.

Colonel Harry B. Liversedge's 28th Marines, 5th Division attacked on VAC's extreme left and were to cut across the narrow neck of the island then turn south-west to secure Mount Suribachi. The 27th Marines, under Colonel Thomas A. Wornham, were to land to the right of the 28th Marines to attack Airfield No. 1 and turn north towards Airfield No. 2. These two Marine regiments were to secure VAC's left flank. The 26th Marines, 5th Division, under Colonel Chester B. Graham, comprised the VAC Reserve to be released on 19 February. The 23rd Marines, 4th Division, led by Colonel Walter W. Wensinger, were to seize Airfield No. 1 and then move northward to Airfield No. 2. The 25th Marines, 4th Division, on the extreme right, were to neutralize the high ground around the 'Quarry' overlooking the East Boat Basin. As Blue Beach 2 was under Japanese gun emplacements in the 'Quarry' overlooking East Boat Basin, it was decided to avoid this landing site and let both the 1st and 3rd Battalions, 25th Marines, 4th Division come ashore abreast on Blue Beach 1. Colonel Walter I. Jordan commanded the 24th Marines as the 4th Division Reserve. Colonel Louis G. DeHaven's 14th Marines (4th Division) and Colonel James D. Waller's 13th Marines (5th Division) comprised the artillery support for the D-Day assault.

Japanese Commanders

In March 1944, the Imperial High Command in Tokyo realized Iwo Jima's importance and began the island's reinforcement. Two months later, 54-year-old Lieutenant General Tadamichi Kuribayashi was summoned by Prime Minister Tojo and placed in command of the IJA 109th Division and tasked with the command of the Iwo Jima garrison, and defend it to the last man. Kuribayashi arrived on Iwo Jima in June 1944 to witness the first USN carrier raids, which nullified Japanese air presence on the island. Kuribayashi knew that without naval and air support, Iwo could not hold out indefinitely against American air and naval supremacy.

To reinforce Iwo Jima, Tokyo dispatched the 145th Infantry Regiment (under Colonel Masuo Ikeda) to Iwo instead of to Saipan; the 5,000 men of the 2nd Mixed Brigade (under Major General Sadasue Senda); the 26th Tank Regiment under Lieutenant Colonel Baron Takeo Nishi; the 17th Mixed Infantry Regiment (under Major Tamachi Fujiwara); a Brigade Artillery Group (under Colonel Chosaku Kaido) that included the artillery battalion of the 2nd Mixed Brigade, the 145th Infantry Regiment's artillery battalion, the 1st and 2nd Mortar Battalions, and the 20th Independent Mortar Battalion. All naval coast defence guns were under the operational control of the Brigade Artillery Group. The brigade was reinforced further by five independent AT battalions, three rocket companies and two independent MG battalions. There were assorted AA (many of which were used primarily as artillery and AT ordnance) and five FA battalions. All of these units were sent to Iwo Jima from Japan via Chichi Jima. Colonel Kaido's artillery HQ was situated in a blockhouse east of Airfield No. 2. Although the IJA units were under Lieutenant General Kuribayashi and Major General Senda and all IJN land forces under Rear Admiral Toshinosuke Ichimaru, the three commanders had separate HQs with cooperation existing between them. By 19 February 1945, Kuribayashi commanded from 21,000 to 23,000 men, including both IJA and IJN units.

Kuribayashi directed his artillery to remain silent during the pre-landing bombardment to conceal their positions. Also, the Marines upon landing were not to encounter any Japanese infantry on the beaches. Once the Marines advanced 500 yards inland, they were to receive concentrated automatic weapons fire from sites on Airfield No. 1 as well as artillery fire from emplacements on the high ground to the north of the landing beaches and from Mount Suribachi to the south. Thus, the Marines, landing craft, equipment and ammunition that had been assembled and crowded together on the beaches would be bombarded from numerous points with all the weapons positioned around the island.

Kuribayashi's intent was a pliable defence while conserving his manpower. His fortifications and ordnance would wear down the Marines and produce excessive American casualties. Kuribayashi inflicted more casualties on the US Marines than his own forces. Also, everything would not be staked on a beachhead attack or futile *banzai* charges. As Kuribayashi's COS in his IJA 109th Division, Colonel Shizuichi Hori, Major General Osuka (CG 2nd Mixed Brigade) along with Captain Samaji Inouye, commander of the Naval Guard Force, all opposed this tactical doctrine for Iwo Jima's defence, a shakeup in command occurred in December 1944. Hori was dismissed as the 109th Division COS and replaced with Colonel Tadashi Takaishi. Also, Major General Osuka was replaced by Major General Sadasue Senda. In all, eighteen Japanese officers were replaced.

Kuribayashi's intricate network of defences and terrain use compelled the Marines to move behind rolling artillery barrages that bombarded well-hidden Japanese strongpoints and then reduce each position with flamethrowers, grenades and demolition charges, making every cave, pillbox and bunker an individual battle.

(**Above**) Admiral Raymond A. Spruance, commander US Fifth Fleet (centre, with arms crossed), who was in overall command of the Iwo Jima campaign, watches the initial air evacuation of wounded, which commenced 3 March. To his left is Rear Admiral Arthur C. Davis, Spruance's COS since September 1944. Davis was a Navy Cross awardee for his command of the USS *Enterprise* during the Battle of the Eastern Solomons on 24 August 1944. (Photo: *Cpl C.L. Warnecke*) (*NARA*)

(**Opposite**) Vice Admiral Richmond Kelly Turner (right) in a command ship's radio shack with a CBS News radio correspondent (far left) and Lieutenant General Holland M. Smith speaking into the microphone. Turner was the Joint Expeditionary Force Commander with Smith the CG Expeditionary Troops. In June 1942, Turner was sent to the Pacific to take command of the Amphibious Force, South Pacific, for the next three years, first as a rear admiral and then vice admiral. He helped plan and execute amphibious operations in the SPA, CPA and western Pacific, including the Solomon, Gilbert, Marshall and Mariana Islands invasions, which for the latter, Vice Admiral Turner was Commander, Joint Expeditionary Force. On 25 May 1945, Turner was promoted to full admiral. (*NARA*)

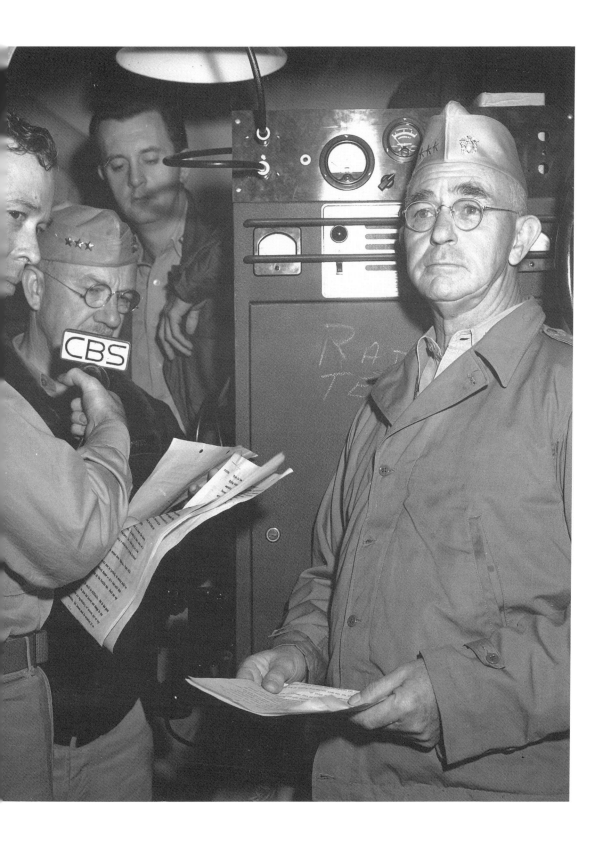

Lieutenant General Holland M. Smith (left), CG Expeditionary Troops, surveys some of the Iwo Jima beachhead carnage with his COS, Colonel Dudley S. Brown, as an LST (right) unloads supplies and vehicles in February. Smith, in his official analysis of the thirty-six-day campaign, wrote, 'There was no hope of surprise, either strategic or tactical. There was little possibility for tactical initiative; the entire operation was fought on what were virtually the enemy's own terms. ... The strength, disposition, and conduct of the enemy's defence required a major penetration of the heart of his prepared positions in the center of the Motoyama Plateau and a subsequent reduction of the positions in the difficult terrain sloping to the shore on the flanks. The size and terrain of the island precluded any Force Beachhead Line. It was an operation of one phase and one tactic. From the time the engagement was joined until the mission was completed it was a matter of frontal assault maintained with relentless pressure by a superior mass of troops and supporting arms against a position fortified to the maximum practical extent.' (NARA)

Marine commanders within a protective shelter as the battle raged. Right to left are: VAC CG Major General Harry Schmidt; Lieutenant General Holland M. Smith, CG Expeditionary Troops (seated at desk); unidentified Marine; Major General Clifton B. Cates, CG, 4th Division; and Brigadier General Franklin Hart, ADC 4th Division. Schmidt was a Fleet Marine, served in China and Nicaragua, and was promoted to major general after serving as COS to the Commandant of the Marine Corps. He took over command of the 4th Division from 18 August 1943 for the Kwajalein invasion in the Marshall Islands (21 January 1944) and Saipan (15 June 1944) during the Mariana Islands campaign, and became VAC CG during the Tinian invasion (12 July 1944). (Photo: *Sgt A.J. Kiely, Jr.*) (*NARA*)

Major General Clifton B. Cates (left), CG 4th Division, Rear Admiral Harry W. Hill (centre), CO Attack Force 58, and Major General Keller E. Rockey (right), CG 5th Division, on Iwo Jima, 12 March. Before the invasion, Cates served as a Marine for twenty-eight years with combat commands at the platoon, company, battalion and division levels. In the First World War, with the 6th Marines at Belleau Wood, Soissons, St Mihiel and Blanc Mont, he received the Navy Cross, two Silver Stars, and two Purple Hearts. He commanded the 1st Marines on Guadalcanal in Major General Alexander A. Vandegrift's storied 1st Division. He took over command of the 4th Division at Tinian. After the war, he became the 19th Commandant of the Marine Corps. Rear Admiral Harry W. Hill was second-in-command, Joint Expeditionary Force, after Vice Admiral Richmond Kelly Turner. Hill was the Attack Force Commander, transporting the 4th and 5th Marine Divisions, and possessed an exact knowledge of the Marines' requirements and equipment cargo handling for the invasion, winning praise from Marine commanders. On 9 March, when Lieutenant General Smith and Vice Admiral Turner departed for Guam, Hill assumed the duties of Senior Officer Present Afloat, Iwo Jima, as Commander Task Group 51.21. Major General Keller E. Rockey had been a Marine for thirty-one years at the time of Iwo's invasion. He also served in France during the First World War, receiving his first Navy Cross in the 5th Marines at Château-Thierry. He won a second Navy Cross for service in Nicaragua before the Second World War. After Pearl Harbor, Rockey was Director, Division of Plans and Policies, then as Assistant Commandant at Marine Corps HQ. In February 1944, he assumed command of the 5th Division and trained that new formation for Operation DETACHMENT. (Photo: *Pvt R. Campbell*) (*NARA*)

Major General Clifton B. Cates, CG 4th Division (centre) is flanked by subordinate officers aboard a transport ship. From left to right are: Colonels John Lanigan (CO, 25th Marines) and Edwin Pollock (Operations Officer 4th Division); Brigadier General Franklin Hart (ADC 4th Divison); Colonels Merton Batchelder (COS 4th Division) and Walter Wensinger (CO, 23rd Marines). Lanigan was a battalion XO, battalion CO and regimental XO, 23rd Marines, at Kwajalein Island in the Marshalls campaign in January 1944, and was wounded on Saipan in June 1944, receiving a Legion of Merit and Navy Presidential Unit Citation. Lanigan would receive a Navy Cross for valour on Iwo Jima. Pollock served as XO, 1st Marines, with Cates as the regimental commander on Guadalcanal in 1942, receiving a Navy Cross and his first Navy Presidential Unit Citation. For the New Britain invasion of December 1943, Colonel Pollock was Assistant COS (G-3) for plans and operations in the 1st Division. Pollock joined Cates in the 4th Division in December 1944 and was the operations officer for the Iwo Jima campaign, receiving a Bronze Star and his second Navy Presidential Unit Citation. Batchelder was CO, 25th Marines, in April 1944, and at Tinian, he helped repel Japanese counterattacks, receiving the Navy Cross and a Navy Presidential Unit Citation. On Iwo Jima, Batchelder was COS, 4th Division, receiving a Bronze Star and another Navy Presidential Unit Citation. Wensinger was a combat veteran with the 4th Division in the Marshall Islands, participating in the capture of the enemy's Roi-Namur airfield, and was awarded a Legion of Merit. During the Mariana Islands campaign, he participated in the capture of Saipan and Tinian, and was awarded a second Legion of Merit. For his valour leading the 23rd Marines on Iwo Jima, he received the Navy Cross. (Photo: *Sgt A.R. Morejohn*) (*NARA*)

In an Iwo Jima 4th Division CP dugout, from left to right, are: Colonel Edwin Pollock, Operations Officer; Colonel Louis De Haven, CO 14th Marines (Artillery); Lieutenant Belk and Lieutenant Colonel Buchanan; with Brigadier General Hart (ADC) and Major General Cates (CG). De Haven's 14th Marines' 1st and 2nd Battalions came ashore on 19 February as the assault regiments were consolidating for night defence. The 3rd and 4th Battalions, 14th Marines, landed on 20 February. (Photo: *SSgt M. Kauffman*) *(NARA)*

Officers of the 4th Division hold a Japanese banner captured at Hill 382 during the 'Meat-grinder' assaults on fortified Japanese positions. The 'Meatgrinder', an enemy master-piece of concealment and construction, confronted Cates's assault battalions, taking seven days to overcome a quartet of Japanese strongpoints; the remnants of Minami Village, the bowl-shaped area referred to as the 'Amphitheatre', 'Turkey Knob' (as dubbed by the Marines), an escarpment of volcanic rock situated 600 yards south of Hill 382 and stood 250 yards north-east of Airfield No. 2, and Hill 382, with its elaborate tunnel system honeycombed with caves, and with light and medium tanks revetted in a maze of ravines and ridges, with Japanese artillery also covering the height. From left to right are Lieutenant Colonel Gooderham McCormick (Intelligence Officer), Colonel Orin Wheeler (Personnel Officer), Colonel Matthew Horner (Logistics Officer), Major General Cates, Brigadier General Franklin Hart (ADC), Colonel Merton Batchelder (Division COS), and Colonel Edwin Pollock (Operations Officer). (Photo: *SSgt M. Kauffman*) *(NARA)*

5th Division leaders exiting a landing beach tent on 21 February, include (left to right): Brigadier General Leo Hermle, ADC (left with hands in pockets), Major General Keller Rockey, CG, smoking cigarette; Colonel James Shaw (Operations Officer) (right of Rockey's left shoulder). Behind and between Hermle and Rockey is Colonel Ray Robinson, COS. Rockey arrived on Iwo this day to establish his HQ near the southern end of Airfield No. 1, captured in part on 20 February. Hermle, a First World War veteran wounded at Verdun in 1918 serving with the 6th Marines, later fought at St Mihiel, Thiaucourt and Blanc Mont, being awarded two Silver Stars while also receiving a DSC and a Navy Distinguished Service Cross during the Meuse–Argonne offensive. In 1942, Colonel Hermle commanded the 6th Marines, 2nd Division, and later as a brigadier general he was ADC for the Tarawa Atoll invasion on 10 November 1943, where he went ashore onto Betio Island to coordinate both defence and arrival of reserve troops, for which he received a Legion of Merit and a Navy Presidential Unit Citation. In January 1944, Hermle was transferred to the VAC staff under Lieutenant General Holland Smith, serving as administrative deputy. In April, he was assigned to the 5th Division as ADC to Major General Rockey. Robinson was a First World War veteran and an ADC to the legendary Marine commander Brigadier General Smedley Butler. In January 1944, Robinson became COS of the 3rd Division and in October 1944, he became COS to the 5th Division for the Iwo campaign. (Photo: *Pvt R. Campbell*) *(NARA)*

Colonel Harry 'The Horse' B. Liversedge, CO 28th Marines, 5th Division, goes over a map of northern Iwo Jima with one of his officers on 8 March. Initially an enlisted private in the Marines, he was commissioned a second lieutenant in September 1918, serving with the 5th Marine Brigade in France. He was a former 1920 and 1924 Olympic track star and a bronze medalist in the 1924 shot put. In January 1942, Lieutenant Colonel Liversedge commanded 2nd Battalion, 8th Marines in American Samoa and in August of that year he assumed command of the 3rd Marine Raider Battalion, leading its unopposed Russell Islands invasion after Guadalcanal in February 1943. Liversedge led the 1st Marine Raider Regiment in the tough jungle of New Georgia Island's west coast in July–August 1943 in the drive to seize Munda Airfield, receiving his first Navy Cross. In January 1944, he was transferred to the 5th Division as CO, 28th Marines, and landed on Iwo on 19 February under murderous Japanese fire. His 28th Marines were tasked with capturing Mount Suribachi and it was one of his units that raised the first and second flags on the summit on 23 February. He was awarded his second Navy Cross for leadership during the thirty-six-day campaign. (Photo: *TSgt B.E. Ferneyhough*) (*NARA*)

(**Above**) At 1645 hours on 24 February, the 9th Marines, 3rd Division came ashore and Major General Graves Erskine established his CP at the northern tip of Airfield No. 1 to take over the central zone of action on 25 February. Erskine was the youngest of the major generals in the Marine Corps. A First World War platoon commander in the 6th Marines, he fought at Belleau Wood, Château-Thierry, Soissons and St Mihiel, during which he was twice wounded, receiving a Silver Star. In the Second World War, Erskine was COS to Lieutenant General Holland Smith during the Aleutians, Gilbert and Marshall Islands campaigns. In October 1944, he became the CG of 3rd Division. During the Iwo campaign, Erskine developed pneumonia but refused evacuation. He had some fractious dialogue with Vice Admiral Kelly Turner and Lieutenant General Holland Smith about landing his 3rd Marines, 3rd Division, which were still afloat, to serve as a replacement unit on 4 March. The other two division commanders concurred with Erskine but Smith and Turner denied Erskine's request. (Photo: *Cpl T.G. Burgess*) *(NARA)*

(**Opposite**) Colonel John B. Wilson, ADC, 3rd Division, points out his troops' front lines in the centre of northern Iwo Jima near the 0-2 Line, on 2 March. By 28 February, the centre and western portions of the VAC front were approaching the 0-2 Line, which extended from Iwo's western coast eastward between Nishi and Hill 362-A, then across northern Iwo Jima between Motoyama Village and the incomplete Airfield No. 3. From there, the 0-2 Line approached the eastern coast at Tachiiwa Point (see map, p. 138). At 0830 hours on 1 March, the 21st Marines, 3rd Division continued the assault with the

2nd and 3rd Battalions abreast of one another after a 12th Marines (Artillery) preparatory bombardment and direct naval gunfire from destroyers, firing from 0800 to 0830 hours. After initial progress, by mid-afternoon these two battalions' forward movement was halted against effective Japanese resistance on high points possessing caves, bunkers and intersecting crevices bristling with assorted defensive weapons of all calibres. At 1540 hours, the 1st Battalion, 9th Marines took over some of the 21st Marines' combat zone. By evening of 1 March, the two 3rd Division regiments were situated 600 yards east of Motoyama Village, running parallel to the incomplete Airfield No. 3. On the morning of 2 March, as indicated on Wilson's 'Special Air and Gunnery Target Map', the 3rd Division continued its attack with the 21st and 9th Marines abreast of one another, but the latter regiment faced strong, well-organised Japanese defences. Likewise, the 21st Marines made only small gains before being halted by MG and AT gunfire from Airfield No. 3. By 1300 hours, the 3rd Battalion, 9th Marines, secured a foothold in front of Hill 362-B against strong Japanese 60mm and 81mm mortar fire, but their advance stalled. Several days transpired before this line of enemy defences was overcome. (Photo: *Cpl T.G. Burgess*) *(NARA)*

(**Above**) Colonel Howard N. Kenyon (left), CO 9th Marines, 3rd Division, examines a map of northern Iwo with his regiment's XO, Lieutenant Colonel Paul W. Russell, on 12 March. By the end of 24 February, Kenyon, a 1921 Naval Academy graduate and Guam combat veteran, led his three battalions into their staging area ashore and were ready to attack at 0700 hours on 25 February, after passing through the 21st Marines, which had been attached to the 4th Division but now were returned to Major General Erskine's 3rd Division for rest and re-equipping. The 9th Marines departed from the south-western edge of Airfield No. 2, after receiving naval gunfire and VAC artillery support, along with USN carrier planes dropping 500lb bombs just before Kenyon's regimental attack began at 0930 hours against Hill PETER – a 360-foot mass of blasted rocks studded with Japanese defences, which was the last major obstacle to secure Airfield No. 2 and its surrounding terrain. Japanese heavy mortar fire ravaged the advancing 9th Marines infantry while some of the 3rd TB M4A2 tanks were set ablaze. By 1400 hours, both the 1st and 2nd Battalions, 9th Marines, made minor gains. When the 3rd Battalion entered the assault, it too began to incur heavy casualties, including many officers from enemy fire, mostly coming from Hill PETER's caves and summit. As 25 February ended, the 9th Marines' line moved north of Airfield No. 2 onto rising ground. Nearly 400 9th Marines fell during their first day of combat and Hill PETER's defenders still fired murderously at Kenyon's men. Nine of the twenty-six M4A2 tanks of the 3rd TB were disabled and seventeen tank crewmen KIA or MIA that day. Kenyon was awarded the Navy Cross for this 25 February action against almost impregnable enemy defences north of Airfield No. 2. (Photo: *SSgt R.R. Robbins*) (*NARA*)

(**Below**) Lieutenant Smith, a platoon leader, gives instructions to Company E, 2nd Battalion, 9th Marines, 3rd Division at 1045 hours on 26 February, as it was to relieve Company G, which sustained heavy casualties. At 0800 hours on 26 February, the 9th Marines resumed the assault after a forty-five-minute artillery barrage against Japanese defences on the major obstacles of Hill PETER and nearby Hill 199 OBOE. The designations Hills PETER and 199 OBOE were derived from target grid locations on the island map and not from elevations, as these hills were actually 360 feet high. Heavy casualties among the 9th Marines and the newly attached 3rd Battalion, 21st Marines, were incurred with slight gains in the high ground north of Airfield No. 2. At 0800 hours on 27 February, the 1st and 2nd Battalions, 9th Marines, again attacked and received withering Japanese mortar, artillery and gunfire from the concealed fortifications on and around Hills 199 OBOE and PETER. Marine armour helped at a cost of eleven M4A2 tanks knocked out. Marine infantry with flamethrowers and bazookas enabled small gains to the base of Hill 199 OBOE and to the top of Hill PETER. Then, a massed VAC and 3rd Division artillery bombardment stunned the Japanese defenders, allowing the 2nd Battalion, 9th Marines, to rapidly advance 1,500 yards into northern Iwo Jima and form a contiguous line with the 1st Battalion, 9th Marines. After the hellacious 25–27 February combat, all of Airfield No. 2 and the high terrain to the north were controlled by the 9th Marines as reduction of bypassed Japanese pillboxes and caves would take two more days. The 21st Marines along with the 3rd TB and 81mm mortar platoons relieved the 9th Marines by 0815 hours on 28 February as Colonel Kenyon's regiment entered 3rd Division reserve. (Photo: *Sgt D.R. Francis*) (*NARA*)

(**Above**) Colonel Hartnoll J. Withers, CO, 21st Marines, 3rd Division (right, with field telephone) at his Yellow Beach regimental CP after landing his three battalions by 1800 hours on 21 February 1945, despite heavy surf. His 21st Marines assembled near the edge of Airfield No. 1 on 21 February, as they were to provide vital assistance in the upcoming task of taking Airfield No. 2. On 22 February, the 21st Marines, 3rd Division was attached to Cates's 4th Division to relieve the 23rd Marines that day. Withers – a 1926 Naval Academy graduate and a Silver Star recipient after leading his 3rd TB, 3rd Division, against the Japanese on Guam on 21 July 1944 – now began to move his 21st Marines in a direct frontal assault against a network of mutually supporting pillboxes on high ground between Airfields Nos. 1 and 2. The terrain was an obstacle for 3rd TB's M4A2 tanks and artillery, making infantry progress slow and costly for the 21st Marines advancing uphill towards Airfield No. 2. (Photo: *Sgt P. Scheer*) (*NARA*)

(**Opposite**) Major Richard Fagan (on field telephone) at his frontline CP after assuming command of the 3rd Battalion, 26th Marines, 5th Division on 22 February after the battalion commander, Lieutenant Colonel Tom Trotti, was KIA. Fagan was awarded the Navy Cross for heroism on 24 February as the 26th Marines advanced 500 yards ahead of his flank supporting units. Fagan directly evaluated his front lines under continuous enemy fire, making the troop positions' adjustments and supervising the distribution of replacements. His unit's casualties that day numbered 21 officers and 332 enlisted men. On 26 February, after waiting for the 3rd Division's advance, the 5th Division resumed its attack with the 26th Marines in the lead, despite heavy enemy fire and hand grenade duels with the Japanese as the terrain became fortified cliffs amid Hill 362-A, situated south-east of Nishi Village, bristling with mortar and MG emplacements in caves. On 26 February, the 26th Marines' 2nd and 3rd Battalions, commanded by Major Amedeo Rea and Major Richard Fagan, respectively, and the 2nd Battalion, 27th Marines, commanded by Major John W. Antonelli, steadily moved towards Hill 362-A. Assisted by M4A3 tanks of the 5th TB, the Marine advance destroyed numerous Japanese guns in the ravines opposite the 26th Marines. (Photo: *Sgt D.G. Christian*) (*NARA*)

(**Above**) The body of Major William R. Day, Operations Officer, 3rd Battalion, 26th Marines, 5th Division, is removed from a crater by three Marines where he and 3rd Battalion CO Lieutenant Colonel Tom Trotti were KIA (as was the battalion sergeant major) by a Japanese mortar round at 0940 hours on 22 February, as Trotti was gradually advancing towards the 0-2 Line. As the 3rd Battalion's XO was already wounded and evacuated, command of the battalion went to Major Richard Fagan, 5th Division Inspector. (Photo: *Sgt D.G. Christian*) *(NARA)*

(**Opposite, above**) Members of the four-man 'Watson Patrol' from Company F, 2nd Battalion, 28th Marines, 5th Division are seen atop Mount Suribachi on 23 February after their reconnaissance was complete. Seated at the left is Sergeant Sherman Watson, while Private Louis Chardo stands in the back with his BAR. Seated in front of Chardo are Privates Theodore White and George Mercer. This patrol preceded the movement of the 3rd Platoon, Company E, 28th Marines, which raised the first 54 × 48-inch flag from the LST USS *Missoula*, led by 1st Lieutenant Harold G. Schrier. (Photo: *Pvt G. Burns*) *(YANK magazine / USAHEC)*

(**Opposite, below**) Major John W. Antonelli gives orders over a SCR-300 ('walkie-talkie') on 1 March. On 19 February, Antonelli led the 2nd Battalion, 27th Marines, 5th Division as it moved inland from Red Beach 1 but ran into heavy Japanese automatic weapon and rifle fire before encountering its first well-camouflaged pillbox 50 yards inland. Companies E and F, trying to cross the island rapidly, bypassed enemy strongpoints which were later neutralized by flamethrower teams and Marine riflemen with hand grenades, along with Marine engineers with HE charges. Antonelli was WIA in the early afternoon of 9 March when a landmine exploded. Also WIA were Lieutenant Colonel Justin G. Duryea, CO 1st Battalion, 27th Marines, and a company commander as they met near the front lines. All the wounded officers were evacuated, with the 1st and 2nd Battalion commands passed to the battalion XOs, Major William H. Tumbleston and Major Gerald F. Russell, respectively. (Photo: *TSgt B.E. Ferneyhough*) *(NARA)*

(**Left**) In June 1944, Japanese Imperial HQ activated the IJA 109th Division and appointed Lieutenant General Tadamichi Kuribayashi (shown above) its CG with overall command of the Iwo Jima garrisons, putting him under the direct command of Tokyo's military leaders. Previously, Kuribayashi served as a deputy military attaché at the Japanese embassy in Washington and studied at Harvard and, like Admiral Yamamoto, became aware of the United States' potential military-industrial might. After the Pearl Harbor raid, he was COS of the IJA Twenty-Third Army occupying Hong Kong. In 1943, he was recalled to Tokyo to be the CG of Second Imperial Guards Home Division with the rank of lieutenant general, a post he held until being given the appointment to fortify Iwo Jima and lead its garrison. He proved to be one of the most competent Japanese field commanders that the Marines ever faced, while displaying leadership qualities of simplicity, economy of force, and maximal use of Iwo Jima's terrain. He directed his subordinate commanders to employ their artillery and mortars with great skill, which exacted a horrific toll on Marine casualties and prohibited senseless squandering of his troops in fruitless suicidal *banzai* charges. (*NARA*)

(**Centre**) Major General Sadasue Senda, commander of the 2nd Mixed Brigade, was a combat veteran with experience in China and Manchuria. Sent to Iwo Jima to assist Kuribayashi with the island's defence, Senda was very well acquainted with artillery and infantry tactics. Kuribayashi created his most elaborate defences across the Motoyama Plateau in the path of the advancing 9th Marines, 3rd Division, with 2nd Mixed Brigade forces comprised of the 310th, 311th and 315th Independent Infantry Battalions, as the major enemy force there. The Japanese had to be driven from the high ground in the centre of Iwo Jima for VAC to open up the western beaches and to get the airfields back into operational status. Senda died on 8 March leading over 400 men in a *banzai* charge against Cates's 4th Division. Approximately half of the Americans KIA during the campaign died in Senda's sector. (*NARA*)

(**Right**) Rear Admiral Toshinosuke Ichimaru, the senior naval officer in command of IJN forces on Iwo Jima. He was one of the foremost airmen in the IJN, having commanded the 27th Air Flotilla in the Tokyo Area. In October 1944, he became commander of the Iwo Jima Naval Guard Force. The next ranking naval officer was Captain Samaji Inoue, also an airman, who commanded the Nanpo Shoto Naval Air Group. (*NARA*)

Gunnery Sergeant John 'Manila John' Basilone sits in a pre-invasion portrait in front of Pacific Ocean maps. Basilone, a Congressional Medal of Honor winner with the 1st Division on Guadalcanal in October 1942, led an MG platoon of the 1st Battalion, 27th Marines, 5th Division past the southern end of Airfield No. 1 on 19 February. Having turned down a commission in favour of remaining in the enlisted ranks, Basilone rushed forward for the island's west coast; however, a Japanese mortar round mortally wounded him and four of his men. (*NARA*)

(**Opposite, above**) 1st Lieutenant Jack Lummus, Company E, 2nd Battalion, 27th Marines, 5th Division, was a graduate of Baylor University, playing varsity football there and later for the New York Giants football team before the war, is shown. On 8 March, Lummus's unit advanced to a jumble of rocks only 150 yards from Iwo's north coast and the sea. Concealed Japanese troops in crevices hindered the Marines' advance to the sea near Kitano Point. Lummus, after fighting for two days and nights without respite, rushed at the head of his rifle platoon to overcome mutually supporting enemy positions as a final obstacle to the sea. Wounded by two grenades, Lummus rushed two Japanese MG emplacements, killing the occupants. His entire company followed his attack leadership until a landmine blew off both legs of the former football star. His Marines continued to advance and by nightfall were on a ridge overlooking the water. Lummus died from his wounds and was awarded a posthumous Congressional Medal of Honor. (*Author's collection*)

(**Opposite, below**) A heavily kitted Private Lloyd Butterfield of the 28th Marines, 5th Division advances up a terrace slope during the inland movement off the beaches on 19 February. The volcanic ash often pulled at the feet of the heavily loaded Marines after only short distances. A mortarman carried 122lb of equipment, while a Navy corpsman about 51lb, with the Marine rifleman carrying packs in between those two weights. (Photo: *Pvt G. Burns*) (YANK *magazine* / USAHEC)

(**Above**) Visible landing beach carnage involves a disabled LVT (A)-4, crushed jeeps, damaged LCVPs and LSM-202. Also apparent was the human cost suffered on the beachhead as a Marine lies dead in the volcanic ash. Navy patrol craft are seen searching the surf for other bodies of fallen Marines. (Photo: *Sgt Mulstay*) (NARA)

(**Opposite, above**) Urgent combat medical support by Navy doctors and corpsmen is rendered in a shell hole to 2nd Battalion, 28th Marines, 5th Division wounded after the initial assault of 19–22 February. Left to right are: USN Lieutenant Dr James Wittmeier, 5th Division Medical Battalion, Navy corpsmen Francis Carroll, Greg Emery, Marion Hall and Seymour March (standing). During that initial fifty-eight-hour post-landing interval, 5,372 Marine casualties were incurred. Elsewhere, at a 1st Battalion, 25th Marines aid station, a Japanese artillery shell directly landed, killing six Navy corpsmen and wounding seven. Unfortunately, 23 Navy doctors and 827 corpsmen were killed or wounded during the Iwo campaign – twice the casualty rate as Saipan. Two wounded Marines are administered plasma, while a deceased Marine (foreground) lies on a litter with a blanket covering his head. (Photo: *WO O. Newcomb*) *(NARA)*

(**Opposite, below**) A corporal in the HQ Company, 1st Battalion, 26th Marines, 5th Division, identified as Corporal W.H. Porter in the official USMC caption, suffered a left leg injury from a Japanese mortar round. He is slid on a poncho into a shell hole on 21 February in preparation to get continued aid at a makeshift beachhead aid station or be transferred by a landing craft to a hospital ship or transport with medical facilities aboard. Rarely had combat medical support been so thoroughly planned as at Iwo Jima. (Photo: *Sgt D. Fox*) *(NARA)*

(**Above**) A dead Japanese soldier west of Airfield No. 2 lays by his weapon, a Type 96 Nambu 6.5mm LMG with a top-mounted, curved thirty-round detachable box magazine and folding bipod, bearing a resemblance to the British Bren LMG. The Type 96 could be fitted with the standard Japanese infantry bayonet, was rugged and reliable, but its 6.5mm bullets lacked penetration capability. It was replaced by the Type 99 LMG, with the larger 7.7mm Arisaka bullet. The Nambu 6.5mm LMG was named after the firearms designer Kijirō Nambu, a general in the IJA and founder of Nambu Arms Manufacturing Company, a major Japanese military firearms maker. Lieutenant General Nambu received the moniker the 'John Browning of Japan'. (Photo: *Sgt D.G. Christian*) *(NARA)*

(**Above**) Two 5th Division corporals, identified as A.R. Cassavant (left) and Thomas McLennon, use a Japanese Hotchkiss HMG to fire at the enemy after their MG was knocked out. The Hotchkiss HMG was developed by Hotchkiss et Cie, established by American gunsmith Benjamin B. Hotchkiss, who emigrated to France in 1867. A number of variants were used by the French Army during the Franco-Prussian War and the First World War, and the interwar years. The Hotchkiss design was used for foreign productions such as the Japanese Type 3 HMG. (Photo: *Sgt J.T. Dreyfuss*) (*NARA*)

(**Opposite, above**) A Marine fires his 0.30-inch calibre 1917A Browning MMG at Japanese positions to support an infantry attack on 19 February. This MMG was capable of delivering high rates of gunfire but was water-cooled to prevent the barrel overheating. Unfortunately, Iwo Jima had a dearth of freshwater so 5-gallon fuel cans with desalinated water were present to cool the barrel. (Photo: *Pfc A.L. Farnum*) (*NARA*)

(**Opposite, below**) A 5th Division rifleman, Sergeant Rinaldo J. Martini of C Company, 27th Marines, carefully aims his M1 Garand 30.06 calibre semi-automatic rifle at Japanese positions from atop enemy ammunition crates in ridge combat in northern Iwo Jima. Sergeant Martini was awarded a Silver Star earlier in the campaign and after the above action, was WIA and evacuated. His M1 Garand rifle was a revolutionary gas-operated, non-bolt-action rifle developed as early as the 1920s by John C. Garand to replace the manually loaded M1903 Springfield rifle. The M1 was the first semi-automatic rifle in military service and helped American soldiers and Marines achieve increased firepower. Its weight was a disadvantage, but it provided a stable platform with relatively low recoil. The M1 magazine was loaded with special clips containing eight rounds. A good rifleman could fire up to thirty rounds per minute. (Photo: *Sgt J.T. Dreyfuss*) (*NARA*)

(**Above**) An intrepid Marine flamethrower from Company E, 2nd Battalion, 9th Marines, 3rd Division runs over the volcanic ash in a crouched posture assaulting a Japanese pillbox at Airfield No. 2 carrying the M2-2 portable version of this weapon. It was introduced in 1944, replacing the M1 model. The M2-2 had two 2-gallon napalm-thickened gasoline fuel tanks and a smaller nitrogen propellant tank fitted onto a metal frame and strapped to his back, with an overall weight of 68lb. (Photo: *Sgt D.G. Christian*) (*NARA*)

(**Opposite, above**) A 9th Marines flamethrower, Private 1st Class Thomas N. Brown, adds new napalm-thickened gasoline fuel to the two larger tanks and nitrogen propellant to the smaller third one (left) of his M2-2 flamethrower between Airfield Nos. 1 and 2 on 27 February. The special ignition cartridges in a revolver-like drum, present at the tip of the flame tube in front of the trigger, replaced the electrical ignition with the earlier M1 model, which had problems requiring the soldier to use his lighter to fire the weapon. (Photo: *Cpl R.G. Simpson*) (*NARA*)

(**Opposite, below**) A Marine flamethrower wearing his M2-2 weapon fires at the entrance of a Japanese pillbox just inland from one of the invasion beaches. Although this weapon had a burn time of seven seconds with usually five bursts and a limited maximal range of 132 feet, it was still quite useful against Japanese pillboxes, dugouts, crevices and cave entrances. As is evident, the flamethrower had to be close to the pillbox's opening, making this task quite hazardous and requiring covering Marine riflemen. (*NARA*)

(**Above**) A Marine flamethrower identified as Private 1st Class Wilfred Voegeli sits still wearing his portable M2-2 weapon strapped to his back on 24 February, with the smoking remnants of a Japanese pillbox behind him. He nonchalantly lights his pipe after having participated in an attack on an enemy fortified position during the 28th Marines' assault on Mount Suribachi. Life expectancy of flamethrowers was extremely truncated due to their reduced speed of movement and the proximity to target that they had to maintain. (Photo: *Pvt R. Campbell*) (*NARA*)

(**Opposite, above**) A forward observation spotter in the 27th Marines, 5th Division, identified as Private 1st Class Alvin C. Dunlap, along with two other Marines examines a grid map, having located an enemy position. Dunlap then calls instructions to be relayed to Marine artillery and mortar units in order to deliver concentrated fire on the Japanese strongpoint. (Photo: *Sgt J.T. Dreyfuss*) (*NARA*)

(**Opposite, below**) A Marine spotter, after observing a Japanese MG position, gives hand signal directions to members of his own MG crew, which had an obscured view of the enemy weapon due to the rocky terrain covered with sparse brush vegetation in northern Iwo Jima on 9 March. (Photo: *Sgt J.T. Dreyfuss*) (*NARA*)

(**Above**) A crew of the 14th Marines (Artillery), 4th Division makes a survey for artillery-men to sight their weapons on Japanese targets on 25 February. Colonel Louis G. De Haven's 14th Marines' 1st and 2nd Battalions landed on 19 February, but once ashore and ready to fire, the 4th Division was consolidating for night defence. The 14th Marines' 3rd and 4th Battalions, except for reconnaissance and survey crews, did not land until

20 February. Heavy enemy fire caused casualties among the men of these reconnaissance and survey teams, one of the first being Lieutenant Colonel Robert E. McFarlane, CO 3rd Battalion, 14th Marines. Fire on the beach became so intense that Colonel De Haven ordered the 3rd Battalion, 14th Artillery reconnaissance party back aboard the fire control ship, but the Marines were unable to get off the beach. (Photo: *Pfc R.R. Dodds*) (*NARA*)

(**Below**) USN surgeons remove mortar fragments from the abdomen of a Marine in the 4th Division hospital far from the front lines. Beyond crude battlefield makeshift aid stations giving first aid, plasma and field dressings, further towards the rear, USN field hospitals arose. Some Marines would be wounded, receive treatment in a field hospital tent, recuperate at a fortified shelter, and return to the front lines only to become wounded again. More seriously wounded Marines would be evacuated off the island, either by air to Guam or on one of many fully staffed hospital ships, while some were too badly wounded to survive either form of evacuation from the island. Within the first month of fighting on Iwo Jima, 13,737 wounded Marines and combat-ready Navy corpsmen were evacuated by ship, while another 2,449 were airlifted off the island. (Photo: *TSgt H.N. Gillespie*) (*NARA*)

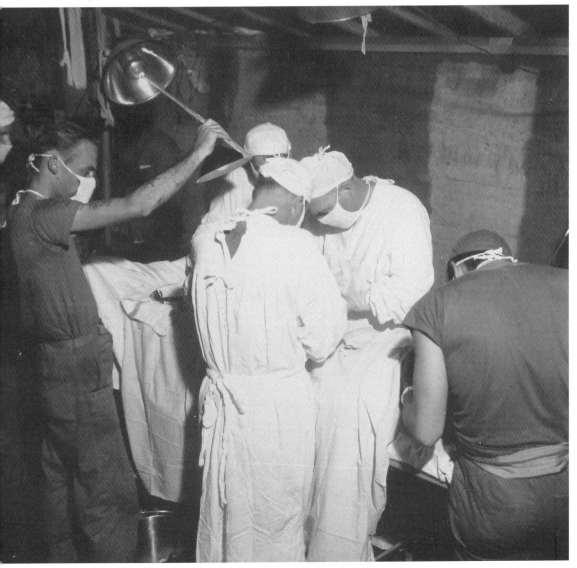

Field communications were better on Iwo Jima than on previous Pacific island assaults. Two Marine wiremen (above) race across an open field without cover while under heavy enemy fire to establish the necessary telephone wire for field communications. Due to the heroic efforts of these Marine signallers, field communications were termed 'near-perfect'. (Photo: *Cpl J. Schwartz*) (*NARA*)

An M29 'Radio Weasel' of the 3rd Division functions at the beachhead on 3 March, with a Marine at the radio set controls and Mount Suribachi looming (left background). A variety of radio systems were utilized on Iwo Jima and almost all were waterproof, with more available frequencies. Forward observer teams used the backpack SCR-610, while companies and platoons preferred the SCR-300 'walkie-talkies' or even the lighter SCR-536 portables. (Photo: *Sgt K.W. Altfather*) (*NARA*)

Two 4th Division Marine signallers repair telephone wires for frontline communications with sulphur fumes emanating from the ground, on 4 March. As the battle progressed, the Marines began stringing telephone lines between support units and forward CPs by elevating the wire along upright posts to avoid damage by tracked vehicles riding over lines on the ground. (Photo: *Sgt N. Ragus*) (*NARA*)

(**Above**) Three 28th Marines, 5th Division Intelligence Section, set up a loudspeaker at Mount Suribachi for a language officer to urge the Japanese to surrender, on 21 February. The few surrendering Japanese were in dire straits and separated from their commanders. When the Japanese did not surrender, men from the 5th Engineer Battalion blasted cave entrances, sealing in enemy soldiers. (Photo: *Sgt L.R. Burmeister*) (*NARA*)

(**Opposite, above**) Marine Navajo Indian 'Codetalkers' are in a shell hole. As the Marines anticipated that Japanese counterintelligence units would splice into American telephone lines, each division employed two dozen trained Navajos, which baffled the Japanese since they could not understand the code. Not one Navajo Codetalker's voice transmission message was broken by the Japanese. The 5th Division CP established six Navajo networks upon arrival on the island. (*NARA*)

(**Opposite, below**) Marine SBs and Navy corpsmen carry a litter with a wounded Marine receiving plasma over rough terrain. Plasma was an essential component for the treatment of wounded soldiers and since red blood cells separated out, there was no need to match the blood type of the donor to the recipient. Dried plasma could be stored for long periods without refrigeration and transported across vast distances. Corpsmen reconstituted the dried plasma with sterile water before transfusion, preventing death from shock. In addition, whole blood of Type O (universal) donors was flown to Iwo Jima by Naval Air Transport Service planes. (Photo: *Pfc J.B. Cochran*) (*NARA*)

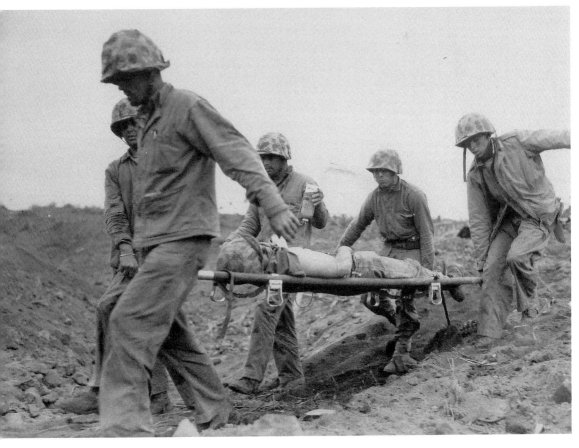

(**Above**) A wounded Marine drags his right leg as two Navy corpsmen assist him. From a frontline casualty clearing station, triage of this Marine would be to a hospital tent area on the island or evacuation to a hospital ship by a landing craft. (Photo: *Sgt D. Fox*) (*NARA*)

(**Opposite, above**) Navy corpsmen infuse plasma to a wounded Marine in a 'Holden Jeep', a modified USMC battlefield ambulance, on 25 February. To transport casualties in the PTO (notably Bougainville, Saipan and Iwo Jima), the USMC turned to General Motors-Holden in Melbourne, Australia, to modify a jeep to have a large medical equipment storage locker in front of the rear tyre normally occupied by a passenger seat. This jeep's design allowed litters to be used for transport instead of Stokes baskets. (Photo: *Sgt A.J. Kiely, Jr.*) (*NARA*)

(**Opposite, below**) Rear view of a 'Holden Jeep' ambulance as it moves along a path next to a Marine bulldozer widening the area to the beach for wounded Marines' evacuation. The jeep's rear door was cut to accommodate the litters and wounded Marines' feet. The Marines were loaded and unloaded by sliding the litter into or out of the channels from the back of the vehicle. Tyre chains are present to negotiate the volcanic sand. (Photo: *SSgt M.A. Cornelius*) (*NARA*)

(**Above**) Six US Army African-American DUKW drivers stand by their 471st Amphibian Truck Company vehicles. They were active throughout the landing. These six almost drowned when their DUKW became swamped with water as the crew attempted to save a drowning Marine. Also, African-American Marines of the 8th Ammunition Company landed on 19 February. Others served as stevedores and stretcher-bearers on the enemy-shelled beaches. On 22 February, the 33rd and 34th Depot Companies, manned by African-American Marines, arrived as part of the VAC shore party. When enemy penetrations of the beachhead occurred, they picked up rifles and engaged the Japanese with 'coolness and courage' and inflicted more casualties than they incurred. Two African-American Marines won Bronze Stars for their gallantry. (Photo: *SSgt W.H. Feen*) (*NARA*)

(**Opposite, above**) An LCVP or LCM crewed by USN sailors and Coast Guardsmen readies for departure from an Iwo landing beach on 25 February, bringing wounded 4th Division Marines to a transport for additional treatment that aid stations near the front lines could not provide. (Photo: *Cpl J. Schwartz*) (*NARA*)

(**Opposite, below**) A B-29 Superfortress crew stands by their crash-landed plane on Iwo Jima after two of its engines were disabled during the 10 March Tokyo Raid. The high price that the Marines paid for the conquest of Iwo Jima from 19 February to 26 March enabled 2,251 damaged or low-on-fuel B-29s and their aircrews to avoid sea crashes. (*NARA*)

Firemen of the USAAF 7th Fighter Command based at Iwo Jima's captured airfields are drenched in foam attempting to extinguish flames from a burning P-51 Mustang as another fighter (above) takes off. Exploding ammunition from the fiery plane drove the firemen away. (*NARA*)

A 4th Division NCO points out a Japanese pillbox to a 4th TB M4A3 tank commander. The M4A3 had a crew of five and, like all the medium tanks in the 4th and 5th TBs, was fuelled with gasoline, unlike the diesel-powered engines of the 3rd TB's M4A2s. Each Marine TB added their own particular type of modification such as wooden planks, metal tank treads or sandbags for added protection. The maximum speed of the M4A3 was 17mph cross-country. The turret housed a 3-inch M3 L/40 75mm cannon while the hull mounted two M1919A4 MGs with a 0.5-inch calibre AA MG positioned on the turret. (Photo: *SSgt M. Kauffman*) (*NARA*)

(**Above**) A Marine M4A3 ('Cairo') of the 4th TB struck a mine, losing a tread. The tank was also hit by Japanese artillery shells upon landing, yet the entire crew survived. The wood planking added to the hull's side prevented suicidal Japanese soldiers from attaching magnetic mines. Steel track links and bogie wheels were mounted on the glacis for additional frontal armour protection from enemy AT weapons. In the turret is Sergeant James W. Reeses. Under the turret's 75mm gun, from left to right, are Corporal Lynn S. Evans and Private 1st Class Lloyd F. Spickate. Charles H. Saulman is examining the damage tread. (*NARA*)

(**Opposite, above**) A Marine patrol passes two M4A3 tanks disabled from Japanese landmines, with Mount Suribachi under bombardment (background) shortly after the landings. The M4 Sherman medium tank was the most commonly used American tank in the Second World War, with more than 50,000 produced from 1942 to 1945. M4 tanks saw combat in North Africa, Italy, and later, Western Europe, but little action in the PTO until 1944, when Japanese reinforced, fixed defences effectively blocked infantry advances using smaller-calibre ordnance. (Photo: *Pvt G. Burns*) (YANK *magazine* / *USAHEC*)

(**Opposite, below**) An M4A3 tank (*Davy Jones*) is reloaded with 75mm ammunition on 22 February. Ammunition was often brought to the tanks and frontline artillery crews by amphibious tractors, jeeps and M29 Weasels. The improved M4A3 tank featured a new large-hatch hull and had a V8 gasoline-powered engine. The thickness of the armour was increased to 2.5 inches. Steel track links were affixed to the turret for additional protection. The M4A3 had ammunition stowed in water and anti-freeze-jacketed bins known as 'wet ammunition stowage', as ammunition racks in earlier M4 prototypes, fitted in the hull sponsons, combusted easily with minor penetrations. (Photo: *Sgt Mulstay*) (*NARA*)

(**Above**) Marine rocket launching trucks of the 3rd Rocket Detachment supporting the 5th Division unleash a barrage of their ordnance before quickly moving to avoid Japanese counterbattery fire on 27 February. A Marine rocket launching truck could fire 8 tons of HE with its complement of (thirty-six) 4.5in rockets over the course of three minutes. On 27 February, the 4th Division's 1st Rocket Detachment blasted Hill 382 with over 500 rockets. (Photo: *WO O. Newcomb*) (*NARA*)

(**Opposite, above**) A 4th Division M2 60mm mortar crew in a natural crevice fires up to eighteen rounds per minute of WP with their high-angle-of-fire weapon, which Marine company commanders used as 'artillery' for close-in ground troop support. A crew of five included squad leader, gunner, assistant gunner and two ammunition carriers. The M2 weighed 42lb and could be assembled quickly. (Photo: *Pfc J.B. Cochran*) (*NARA*)

(**Opposite, below**) A Marine M1 81mm mortar (weighing 134lb) crew fires rounds at Mount Suribachi from a reinforced pit dug into volcanic ash on 20 February as the 28th Marines, 5th Division began their assault on the mountain. The 81mm mortar provided a more sustained and greater range of indirect fire support for Marine assault troops than the 60mm mortar. Its crew of eight included: squad leader, gunner, assistant gunner, and five ammunition carriers. It could fire up to a maximum of thirty to thirty-five rounds per minute with maximum firing range of 3,300 yards. (*NARA*)

(**Above**) A Marine M3 37mm AT cannon fires at Mount Suribachi from its gun pit with a bulldozer (right), on 21 February. This gun was introduced in 1937; however, by 1941 it was considered obsolete in the ETO so it was deployed to the PTO until the war's end for Marine and Army ground forces' use. Due to Pacific island terrain and jungle, the light weight of this weapon was advantageous as it did not require a vehicle for towing. Although this crew used HE rounds against Japanese fortifications, delaying the 28th Marines' advance at Mount Suribachi, this gun also fired a canister, which was capable of breaking up enemy infantry attacks. (Photo: *SSgt M.A. Cornelius*) (*NARA*)

(**Opposite, above**) Amtracs burn from Japanese mortar and artillery fire on the beachhead with Mount Suribachi looming (background). A Marine M8 75mm pack howitzer (foreground) stands in a shallow gun pit with sandbags (left foreground). The 1st Battalion, 14th Marines (Artillery), had eleven 75mm pack howitzers off their landing craft by 1715 hours on 19 February and manhandled up the sand terraces, and were ready for firing within thirty minutes, providing the assaulting Marines with close-fire support. The 75mm pack howitzer provided a mobility advantage over larger fieldpieces, having a 'box trail' design and rubber wheels for jeep transport. (*NARA*)

(**Opposite, below**) An M8 75mm pack howitzer with a six-man gun crew in a sandbagged position on 7 March is readied for firing. Originally for mountain divisions or units that needed a light but effective howitzer, which could be transported by gun crews or pack animals, the M8 weighed 1,270lb and could be dismantled and carried in six separate parts, the heaviest weighing 220lb. It could be reassembled by a trained crew in three minutes and at Iwo Jima, it was brought to the beachhead by LCVPs, DUKWs and amphibious tractors, and carried inland by a variety of vehicles. This gun had a range of 9,500 yards as it hurled a 14lb HE shell at a firing rate of three to six rounds per minute. The tube could elevate to 45 degrees and depress to –5 degrees with a 6-degree traverse. Its dimensions were 13 feet long, 4 feet wide, and just over 3 feet high. (*NARA*)

(**Opposite, above**) A 3rd Battalion, 14th Marines (Artillery), M2A1 105mm M2 howitzer is situated in a sandbagged, wood-reinforced pit for firing onto Mount Suribachi. On 19 February, the 105mm howitzers of the 2nd Battalion, 14th Marines (Artillery), unable to be manhandled, required their DUKWs to move them over the terrace. By dusk on D-Day, all twelve 105mm howitzers were in position near Yellow Beach 1. This gun had a split trail mount and weighed 4,500lb, and fired HE shells a maximum range of 37,350 feet. It could be elevated to 65 degrees and depressed to –5 degrees, with a 46-degree traverse. (*Sgt Mulstay*) (*NARA*)

(**Opposite, below**) Marine engineers and Naval 'Seabees' build roads and unload supplies at the beachhead. It was said that Marines returning to the beaches from northern Iwo could hardly recognize what they had fought through and left on 19 February. With more than 80,000 Americans ashore, roads and infrastructure were necessary to continue the combat. (*NARA*)

(**Above**) USN doctors and corpsmen at a 3rd Medical Battalion aid station deliver care to Marine casualties in a former Japanese concrete shelter at Airfield No. 1. The wounded Marines on the litters are receiving plasma infusions. The Navy corpsman (centre) is writing a brief description of the wounds and treatment given in the event of later evacuation to another facility. (Photo: *TSgt J.A. Mundell*) (*NARA*)

(**Above**) US Coast Guardsmen provide assistance to bring aboard a dazed, wounded Marine amphibious tractor crewman whose vehicle was hit and disabled at sea. The USCG LCVP was designed for rescue, repair and evacuation of assault craft offshore. The USCG landed Marine divisions along with their gear, bulldozers, vehicles, rations, small arms, water and virtually everything needed to keep the assault moving inland, as well as evacuate wounded Marines. Many members of the USCG, who served at Iwo as coxswains and crew members of assault craft as well as on LST, LCMs and LCIs, were veterans of the Normandy invasion of 6 June 1944. (*NARA*)

(**Opposite, above**) 3rd Division Japanese-American *Nisei* interpreters Corporal T. Tora-kawa (left) and Staff Sergeant E. Kawamata (right) in their foxhole in February. More than fifty Military Intelligence Service (MIS) *Nisei* linguists were among the three Marines divisions on Iwo Jima. MIS was not a unit, like the 100th Infantry Battalion and 442nd Infantry Regiment in the ETO; however, it provided thousands of intelligence and language specialists, usually in small teams with Army, Navy, Marine Corps and Allied units throughout the Pacific and CBI theatres, as well as in the Aleutian Islands. They listened to Japanese radio communications, pored over captured documents for information, and questioned captured Japanese troops. (Photo: *Cpl R. Impenachio*) (*NARA*)

(**Opposite, below**) At a 9th Marines, 3rd Division CP, MIS *Nisei* linguist Technical Sergeant Terry Takeshi Doi (right), cradling an M1 semi-automatic carbine rifle, ques-tions captured Koreans in March. Doi landed on 19 February and was one of more than fifty MIS linguists who fought alongside the Marines. He was awarded a Silver Star after entering cave after cave to persuade Japanese soldiers to surrender. The War Department Intelligence Division sought to train Japanese-American *Nisei* on the West Coast as

Japanese language interpreters and translators. At the war's outbreak, over fifty students trained at the US Army's Presidio in San Francisco, and when thirty-five graduated, they were sent overseas for the Guadalcanal and Papua campaigns. In 1942, the War Department renamed the programme the Military Intelligence Service (MIS) Language School after it was relocated to Fort Snelling, Minnesota. By the time of the Saipan invasion, there were 1,200 graduates of the school. (Photo: *SSgt R.R. Robbins*) (*NARA*)

A *Nisei* language officer of the MIS with the 4th Division tries to coax Japanese soldiers to surrender at the mouth of an Iwo Jima cave entrance. Marine intelligence gathering efforts were hampered by the tendency for frontline Marines not to take prisoners. So MIS language specialists resorted to offering rewards such as bottles of soda or ice cream to Japanese troops who brought in live prisoners for questioning. Only 1,000 of the more than 20,000 Japanese defenders surrendered with the assistance of the MIS, who entered caves urging the enemy to surrender rather than commit suicide. (Photo: *Pfc J.B. Cochran*) (*NARA*)

A Japanese soldier who has surrendered is questioned at a frontline cave by an MIS *Nisei* linguist (right) and accompanying Marines. For each combat operation, teams of enlisted *Nisei* MIS linguists and translators, led by Caucasian officers, shared frontline hardships with the combat troops. Some fell ill with malaria, dysentery and other hazards of the tropics; some were KIA or WIA. MIS *Nisei* translators constantly risked being mistaken for the enemy and were regularly assigned bodyguards. In regards to the questioning of POWs, Japanese troops were not trained to resist interrogation. Nor were they barred from keeping diaries and letters, which, when captured, provided priceless information. (Photo: *Cpl E. Jones*) (NARA)

(**Above**) Interrogators from the 9th Marines, 3rd Division question a talkative Japanese prisoner holding a cigarette in the rocky northern sector of Iwo Jima, in March. In the Solomon Islands and on New Guinea, MIS linguists learned that humane treatment and sympathetic questioning of Japanese POWs yielded far more information than harsh interrogation methods. (Photo: *Sgt R.R. Robbins*) *(NARA)*

(**Opposite, above**) 4th Division Marine stretcher-bearers armed with M1 0.30-in calibre semi-automatic carbine rifles advance under fire through a recessed track with some vegetation for cover to rescue a wounded Marine. A Japanese soldier who refused to surrender lies dead at the right. The Japanese warrior or *bushido* code expected the Emperor's soldiers to either win or die. A 4th Division Intelligence officer on 10 March summed up the enemy's morale as 'disorganized but his will to fight to the death is undiminished'. (Photo: *Sgt A.R. Morejohn*) *(NARA)*

(**Opposite, below**) Marine Corporal Virgil Burgess and his courier dog Prince of either the 6th or 7th War Dog Platoon is about to deliver a message to another foxhole one week after the 19 February invasion. The message pouch is strapped around the dog's back. The majority of the first dogs shipped overseas (the 1st War Dog Platoon) were Doberman Pinschers, the remainder German and Belgian Shepherds, and they arrived in the South Pacific on 11 July 1943 and went into combat on Bougainville with the 2nd Marine Raider Regiment (Provisional) in November 1943. Half the animals were trained as messenger dogs, with the other half as scout dogs. *(NARA)*

A 6th or 7th War Dog Platoon patrol comprised of three Doberman Pinschers and their Marine handlers moves out. A War Dog Platoon was assigned to a Marine regiment with a regimental staff officer serving as advisor in the use of dogs as well as commanding the platoon comprised of sixty-five men, and thirty-six dogs (eighteen messenger and eighteen scout). It was generally believed that the shorthaired Doberman was more adaptable to the heat of the tropics than many of the longer-haired breeds. Marine dog handlers were unanimous in their praise of the Doberman Pinscher and the German Shepherd for scout and messenger work. (*NARA*)

A new Marine dog handler in the 25th Marines, 4th Division, Private 1st Class Rez P. Hester rests under a poncho in a volcanic sand foxhole. His 7th War Dog guard, Butch, a Doberman Pinscher, sits attentively by his side on alert for any Japanese infiltrators of the Marine lines as well as signalling to Marines the presence of landmines and 'booby traps'. By providing security, the dogs reduced Marine casualties; however, Butch's previous Marine handler was WIA. (*NARA*)

Chapter Four

The Landings and Capture of Airfield No. 1

At 0902 hours on 19 February 1945, the first wave of LVT (A)s of the 5th Division's 28th and 27th Marines landed at Green and Red Beaches, respectively, while those of the 4th Division's 23rd and 25th Marines assaulted Yellow and Blue Beaches. At 0905 hours, the second wave (first of the troop-carrying waves) emerged from the water. Within minutes of landing, Japanese mortar, artillery and machine-gun fire raked the Marines on the volcanic ash and approaching incoming waves of amphibious tractors and LCVPs from positions in Mount Suribachi's caves, as well as mutually supporting blockhouses and pillboxes. Nonetheless, Marines and supplies continued to come ashore as all eight assault battalions were at the beachhead ashore within ninety minutes of the first wave's landing. Between 1005 and 1020 hours, LSMs transporting 4th and 5th TB M4A3s landed their armour but the medium tanks had difficulty getting ashore, while others hit Japanese landmines just yards from the water's edge. Some M4A3 medium tanks fired their 75mm turret guns to neutralize Japanese pillboxes beyond the beach.

5th Division's Inland Advance after Landings

The 28th Marines were to isolate and assault Mount Suribachi after landing with its 1st Battalion cutting across the island's narrow neck (achieved by 1035 hours), while the 2nd Battalion advanced inland and southward towards the volcano (codenamed HOTROCKS). The 3rd Battalion, 28th Marines landed from division reserve at 1300 hours, incurring many casualties on the run-in. By 1545 hours, the 2nd and 3rd Battalions, 28th Marines, with 5th TB armour, advanced but tanks were again hampered by the soft volcanic ash and the mined sand terraces.

After the 1st and 2nd Battalions, 27th Marines landed at Red Beach. Some companies by 1130 hours, after bypassing many enemy positions, moved across Airfield No. 1's southern end and then up along the western edge of the airstrip. Another company moved north-westerly from the south-western end of the field. The 26th Marines, the 5th Division's reserve regiment, was released by VAC just before 1000 hours, with its 1st Battalion ashore by 1500 hours. Overcoming heavy casualties, the 5th Division established a 1,500-yard-wide by 1,000-yard-deep beachhead, dividing the northern from the southern part of the island and isolating the Mount Suribachi sector. Their front lines were also astride the southern aspect of Airfield No. 1. At 1430 hours, Brigadier General Hermle, 5th Division ADC, the first general on Iwo, crossed Airfield No. 1 under Japanese gunfire, gathering intelligence from frontline Marines and setting up an advanced division CP. By 1744 hours, the 5th Division's assault regiments consolidated for the night south of Airfield No. 1.

4th Division's Inland Advance

Colonel John R. Lanigan's 1st and 3rd Battalions, 25th Marines secured the northernmost Blue Beaches. However, heavy casualties, including officers, were incurred. The 25th Marines' reserve 2nd Battalion was tasked to move north-west and seize high ground near 'The Quarry' to assist the 3rd Battalion movement in order to close the gap between the 1st and 3rd Battalions. By early evening, the 2nd and 3rd Battalions seized the high ground inland of 'The Quarry' but with staggering casualties, as the combat strength of the 3rd Battalion, 25th Marines, was reduced to only 150 riflemen.

The 4th Division's reserve, the 1st and 2nd Battalions, 24th Marines (CO Colonel Walter I. Jordan), landed on Yellow Beach 2 at 1700 hours to relieve Cates's battered battalions and to take up nocturnal defensive positions just short of the airfield by 2400 hours. The 3rd Battalion, 24th Marines (the last of the divisional reserve, CO Lieutenant Colonel Alexander A. Vandegrift, Jr.) landed before 1900 hours and moved just inland from Blue Beach 2 before digging in preparation of an anticipated Japanese counterattack. The 4th Division reached a line extending northward to 'The Quarry' atop the ridge for 300 yards and southward across low ground towards the main runway of Airfield No. 1, as Lieutenant Colonel Chambers 3rd Battalion, 25th Marines took possession and held this rocky height at a cost of 750 casualties.

By nightfall of 19 February, VAC landed six infantry regiments, six artillery battalions, and tons of equipment to support the approximately 30,000 men ashore. The 4th and 5th Division troops were nowhere near the 0-1 Phase Line (see map, p. 140) except at 'The Quarry'. The D-Day casualty count was 501 Marines KIA; 1,775 wounded in action; 47 dying from their wounds and 18 MIA. Many of those killed or injured fell victim during the overnight Japanese shelling of the congested Marine beachhead exemplified on Yellow Beach 1, where the 1st Battalion, 23rd Marines CP received a direct hit, which killed the CO, Lieutenant Colonel Haas, and his G-3 (Operations Officer) Captain Fred C. Eberhardt. However, much of the Japanese heavy artillery on Mount Suribachi's slopes was eliminated by pre-invasion aerial and naval bombardment, although enemy ordnance elsewhere continued a steady barrage of VAC positions.

Capture of Airfield No. 1

At 0830 hours on 20 February, VAC attacked to the north after a massive bombardment. In the 5th Division sector, Colonel Thomas A. Wornham's 3rd Battalion, 27th Marines (CO Lieutenant Colonel Donn J. Robertson) and 1st Battalion, 26th Marines (CO Lieutenant Colonel Daniel C. Pollock) advanced slowly due to enemy pillboxes, landmines, mortar and artillery fire, and AA gun rounds as the other two 27th Marines' battalions were in reserve. M3A3 tanks from two companies of the 5th TB accompanied the Marines, who were taking heavy casualties. By 1800 hours, after gaining 800 yards, Wornham ordered the two battalions to dig in along a line running east to west from the north-western edge of Airfield No.1 to the island's west coast.

Also at 0830 hours on 20 February, the 4th Division's 23rd and 25th Marines attacked, with the 1st Battalion, 25th Marines (CO Lieutenant Colonel Hollis U. Mustain, who would be KIA the next day) on the left making the main effort with the 2nd Battalion, 25th Marines in the centre (CO Lieutenant Colonel James Taul replacing the battalion CO, Lieutenant Colonel Lewis C. Hudson, Jr., who was KIA earlier on 20 February) seizing the high ground to its front and supporting the 1st Battalion. The 1st Battalion, 24th Marines (attached to the 25th Marines under the command of Major Paul S. Treitel), remained stationary until the 1st and 2nd Battalions, 25th Marines, became aligned after their attack. The 3rd Battalion, 25th Marines (CO Lieutenant Colonel Justice Chambers, who would be WIA on 22 February), remained in regimental reserve, recovering from their heavy D-Day losses.

By noon, the 3rd Battalion, 23rd Marines swept past the northern part of Airfield No.1, gaining 500 yards, incurring severe casualties from enemy pill-boxes and infantry strongpoints, as the 1st and 2nd Battalions, 23rd Marines moved along the airfield's eastern edge. By nightfall, the 23rd Marines were in direct contact with the 27th Marines, 5th Division on the left and the 25th Marines on the right. By nightfall of 20 February, Airfield No.1 was completely captured as Marine units dug to consolidate their day's gains of 200 to 300 yards. The price in Marine blood to capture Airfield No.1 was exorbitant, with the 5th Division losing 1,500 men KIA and WIA, and the 4th Division 2,000 men.

Wrecked enemy planes at the edge of Airfield No.1, 21 February 1945.
(Photo: *Pvt G. Burns*) (YANK *magazine / USAHEC*)

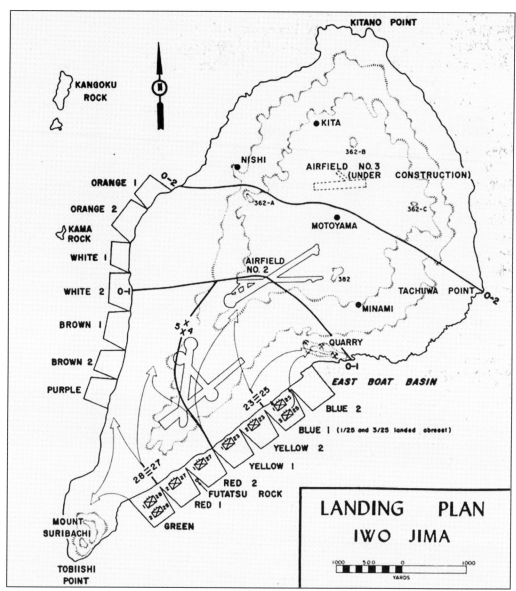

KITANO POINT

KANGOKU ROCK

KITA

362-B

NISHI

AIRFIELD NO. 3 (UNDER CONSTRUCTION)

ORANGE 1

O-2

ORANGE 2

362-A

KAMA ROCK

MOTOYAMA

362-C

WHITE 1

AIRFIELD NO. 2

WHITE 2

O-1

382

TACHIWA POINT

O-2

MINAMI

BROWN 1

3 x
x 4

BROWN 2

QUARRY

O-1

EAST BOAT BASIN

PURPLE

23≡25

BLUE 2

BLUE 1 (1/25 and 3/25 landed abreast)

YELLOW 2

28≡27

YELLOW 1

RED 2

FUTATSU ROCK

RED 1

MOUNT SURIBACHI

GREEN

TOBIISHI POINT

LANDING PLAN

IWO JIMA

1000   500   0   1000
YARDS

(**Above**) A map of the Iwo Jima Landing Plan for 19 February 1945, with the main beaches on the eastern coast and the principal locales including Mount Suribachi, the airfields, the 0-1 and 0-2 Phase Lines (created by VAC commander Major General Harry Schmidt), the northern villages (Minami, Motoyama, Nishi and Kita) and the heavily fortified Hills 362-A, B and C, and Hill 382. (*USMC*)

(**Opposite**) A map shows Iwo Jima's five Japanese defence sectors with troop positions. The Mount Suribachi sector had casemated CD artillery, automatic weapons in mutually supporting pillboxes defended by IJA 312th Independent Infantry Battalion, along with IJN AA units. A main cross-island defence line of broken terrain, in-depth pillboxes, bunkers, blockhouses and dug-in immobilized tanks extended across Iwo's mid-section, from the north-west cliffs across Airfield No. 2 to Minami Village in the east and then further eastward to the shoreline just south of Tachiiwa Point. A secondary line of defence extended across northern Iwo, across the incomplete Airfield No. 3, the Motoyama plateau and village, and then to the eastern shore containing fewer Japanese constructed fortifications but numerous natural caves and other terrain features. Airfield Nos. 1 and 2 were protected from direct assault by AT ditches near the runways and the mining of all approach routes. The Western Sector fielded units of the IJA 311th Independent Infantry Battalion, the IJA 1st Company, 26th Tank Regiment, and a Naval Landing Force (NLF) unit trained and equipped as infantry. Although not assigned to a specific defence sector, the IJA 1st Battalion, 145th Infantry Regiment, occupied Airfield No.1 area. The Southern Sector fielded the IJA 309th Independent Infantry Battalion, an NLF unit, and IJN AA and CD units. The Eastern Sector was defended by the IJA 314th Independent Infantry Battalion, the IJA 3rd Company, 26th Tank Regiment, and IJN AA and CD units. In the Northern Sector was Lieutenant General Kuribayashi's redoubt HQ towards the end of the campaign. There was also the IJA 3rd Battalion, 17th Independent Mixed Regiment, the IJA 2nd Company, 26th Tank Regiment, an SNLF unit and IJN AA and CD units. (*USMC*)

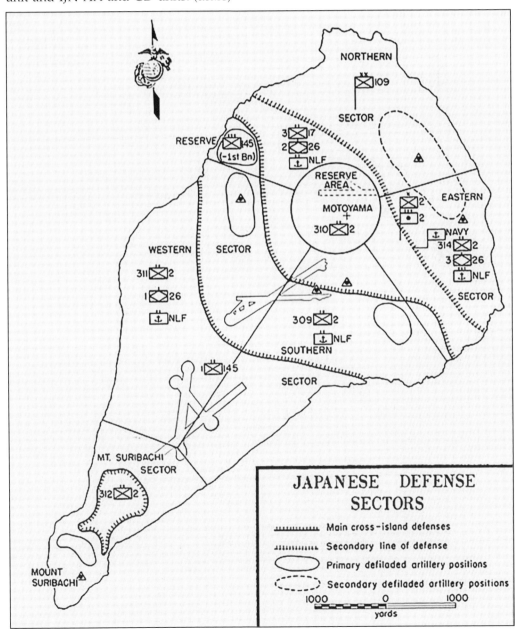

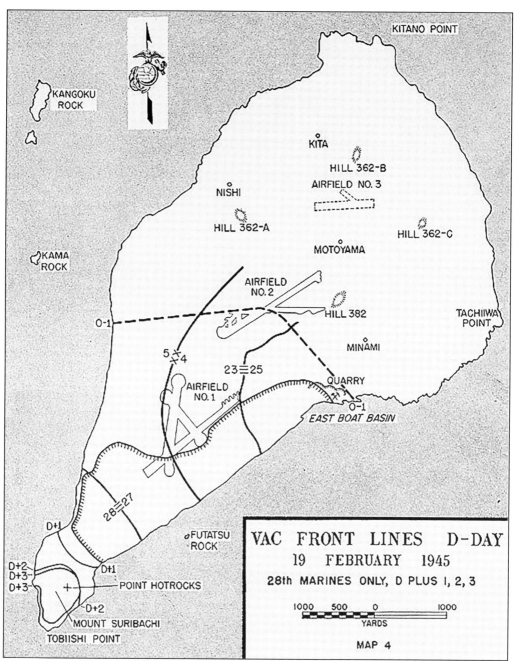

KITANO POINT

KANGOKU
ROCK

KITA

HILL 362-B

AIRFIELD NO. 3

NISHI

HILL 362-A

HILL 362-C

KAMA
ROCK

MOTOYAMA

AIRFIELD
NO. 2

0-1

HILL 382

TACHIIWA
POINT

5 ✕ 4

MINÁMI

23 ≡ 25

QUARRY

AIRFIELD
NO. 1

0-1

EAST BOAT BASIN

28 ≡ 27

D+1

FUTATSU
ROCK

D+2
D+3
D+3

D+1

POINT HOTROCKS

D+2

MOUNT SURIBACHI

TOBIISHI POINT

VAC FRONT LINES D-DAY
19 FEBRUARY 1945
28th MARINES ONLY, D PLUS I, 2, 3

1000   500   0   1000

YARDS

MAP 4

A map depicting the VAC front lines at the end of D-Day, 19 February, which reached the south-western and eastern edges of Airfield No. 1, extending to a ridge atop 'The Quarry' captured by units of the 25th Marines, 4th Division. The forward advance of only the 28th Marines attacking Mount Suribachi is enumerated as D+1, D+2, D+3 and D+4, as Colonel Liversedge's battalions first surrounded and then scaled Mount Suribachi. However, the 0-1 Phase Line, which was not reached on 19 February, indicated initial objectives and delineated commanding or conspicuous terrain features where units could be halted for control, coordination and further orders. It extended from the island's west coast eastwards, through the mid-portion of Airfield No. 2, and curved south-eastwards to 'The Quarry' to the north of the East Boat Basin. (*USMC*)

Early on 19 February, Rear Admiral Hill's TF 53 assault vessels, carrying the 4th and 5th Divisions, joined Rear Admiral William H.P. Blandy's Amphibious Support Force, forming the largest armada for a PTO island invasion, with a hazy Mount Suribachi (left background). The transports carrying 50,000 Marines were 10,000 yards offshore with favourable weather. At 0640 hours, the gun crews of the USS *North Carolina*, *Washington*, *New York*, *Texas*, *Arkansas* and *Nevada*, comprising Rear Admiral Rogers's Gunfire and Covering Force along with gunboat, rocket and mortar support ships, commenced the pre-H-Hour bombardment tasked to silence the Japanese guns that dominated the assault boat lanes, and blasted the landing beaches, airfields and northern portion of Iwo Jima, with the latter's numerous ridges and gullies. (Photo: *Sgt H.N. Gillespie*) (*NARA*)

(**Above**) 5th Division Marines leave their transport to board their LCVP at 0725 hours for the run-in to the beachhead, with their faces covered with anti-flash cream. Sergeant William Genaust (without anti-flash cream), a 5th Division combat cinematographer, stands behind the cannon. Thirty minutes later, eight battalions of Marines were carried towards the shore in LCVPs and amphibian tractors. (Photo: *Pvt R. Campbell*) (*NARA*)

(**Opposite, above**) At 0825 hours, the naval bombardment, including 5-inch destroyer and 8-inch cruiser guns, resumed directed gunfire against only the landing beaches with 8,000 shells. Rolling barrages with destroyers' 5-inch guns were to be timed with the Marines' inland advance. (*NARA*)

(**Opposite, below**) An LST heads for the beachhead on 19 February, dwarfing amphibious tractors flanking it. Mount Suribachi looms (left background) with the 5th and 4th Divisions' landing beaches to the mountain's north (right background). USN warships and control vessels on station completed landing beach bombardment and formed a line of departure for the Marines' amphibious vessels, respectively. (Photo: *Pfc R.R. Dodds*) (*NARA*)

From the interior of a USCG-crewed LST, an amphibious tractor becomes waterborne to join the nearby landing craft forming up to assault the beaches. The Coast Guardsman on the LST bow ramp gives an encouraging hand signal to the departing Marines. *(NARA)*

At 0815 hours on 19 February, the first of ten waves of Marines travelling 4,000 yards from the transports to cross the line of departure to the eastern landing beaches, with each successive wave separated at 250 to 300 yards and five-minute intervals. The line of departure for the landing craft was 2 miles offshore, ran parallel to the beaches, and had USN control vessels marking the boundary. The LVT (A)-4s of the first landing wave, with their M8 howitzer turrets, hit the volcanic ash at 0902 hours and tried to move inland to neutralize enemy positions, although sand terraces up to 15 feet high obscured Japanese gunfire. Some of these LVT (A)-4s returned from the volcanic ash to the water to provide cover fire for the now-landing Marines since at 0905 hours, the second wave of landing craft (the first troop-carrying LCVPs) lowered their ramps after emerging from the water, enabling the Marines to hit the volcanic ash at a run. The plan was to land 9,000 Marines in less than forty-five minutes. A few isolated artillery and mortar shells began to land in the water's edge as later waves approached and the beaches became congested. There were only land mines, and no other Japanese beach obstacles. (NARA)

(**Above**) Low-level carrier-borne Curtiss SB2C Helldiver dive-bomber aircraft bomb enemy targets 500 yards inland from the beach as the first Marine wave landed. After the naval bombardment ceased just after 0800 hours, over 100 USN fighters and bombers, including F4U Marine Corsairs and F6F Hellcats of TF 58, attacked Mount Suribachi, the landing beaches and the high ground to the landing beaches' north. Some Mariana Islands-based USAAF bombers arrived to drop 20 tons of 100lb bombs on eastern Iwo Jima's defences. (*NARA*)

(**Opposite, above**) Several LVT (A)-4s with 3-inch, short-barrelled 75mm M3 howitzer guns placed in an HMC M8 howitzer turret, form the first landing wave (middle). Sixty-eight of these tracked vehicles landed at 0902 hours on 19 February to provide immediate fire support for the subsequent landing craft carrying the 30,000 Marines of the 4th and 5th Divisions after naval gunfire lifted and until artillery units landed and were ready to fire. Previous island landings noted the insufficient fire support by the 37mm M6 tank gun of the LVT (A)-1. Mount Suribachi is seen through the gunsmoke (left background) with a USN cruiser in front of the volcano firing its 8-inch guns at Japanese positions. (Photo: *SSgt G.B. Kress*) (*NARA*)

(**Below**) LCVPs with some of the assault troops of the eight Marine Infantry Battalions from the 4th and 5th Divisions are in line to land at their respective beaches on Iwo Jima's eastern coast just north of Mount Suribachi (centre background) and south of East Boat Basin. Small USN control vessels (background) and a destroyer (right) are at the line of departure. (Photo: *Associated Press photographer Joe Rosenthal*) (*NARA*)

(**Opposite, above**) Marines of the 4th Division land and advance up the volcanic ash as ammunition carts are dragged out of the surf (left) and from the LCVP (right), while others climb a small sand terrace. (Photo: *Associated Press photographer Joe Rosenthal*) (*NARA*)

(**Opposite, below**) Marine riflemen of the 4th Division from a later wave clamber out of their LCVP to ascend a small sand terrace and witness some of the carnage at the beachhead caused by the commencement of Japanese artillery and mortar fire that had been silent for the first assault waves' arrival. A disabled vehicle, probably an LVT (A)-4, is stranded (right foreground) while a 15-foot high sand terrace (background) impedes both divisions' assault forces and amphibious tractors. (Photo: *TSgt H.N. Gillespie*) (*NARA*)

(**Above**) Coast Guard coxswains and LCVP crewmen in a later 4th Division wave witness the stalled beachhead advance. Marines burrowed into a sand terrace while awaiting orders to move forward. To their front, small 4th Division Marine units and LVT (A)-4 amphibious tractors moved forward towards a foreboding plateau towards Airfield No. 1 but in the process are receiving heavy Japanese artillery, AA gunfire, mortar and small-arms fire. By 1000 hours, LSMs brought sixteen M4A3 tanks from Company C, 4th TB, to the Yellow 1 and 2 Beaches. Even as some of the M4A3 tanks proceeded inland, aid to the 2nd Battalion, 23rd Marines was hindered. The 1st Battalion, 23rd Marines received limited armoured support to assist its advance. An attempt to retrieve the disabled tanks and tractors was hampered by the terrain and heavy mortar and artillery fire. (Photo: *TSgt H.N. Gillespie*) (*NARA*)

(**Above**) Three 5th Division Marines, carrying packs and holding their M1 Garand rifles, drag a cart while under enemy fire through the surf and onto the soft volcanic sand from their LCVP (right) at Green Beach at 1616 hours on 19 February. The Japanese defenders employed entrenched guns as heavy as 150mm against the assault waves approaching the shoreline as the dense network of artillery positions was hidden in caves, tunnels and behind reinforced steel doors within Mount Suribachi. (Photo: *Sgt D.G. Christian*) *(NARA)*

(**Opposite, above**) The 2nd Battalion, 27th Marines (CO Major John W. Antonelli) lands at Red Beach 1 during the afternoon of 19 February, with Mount Suribachi shrouded in gunsmoke (background). Colonel Thomas A. Wornham's 27th Marines started their advance from Red 1 and 2 Beaches, where the 1st and 2nd Battalions landed abreast of one another. Casualties mounted from Japanese artillery and mortar fire as they advanced, including Colonel Louis Plain, the XO of the 27th Marines, who was evacuated and replaced by Lieutenant Colonel James Berkeley. The southern end of Airfield No. 1 was approached by the 1st Battalion, 27th Marines at 1130 hours, with further consolidation along the western edge of the field. The remnants of Company A, 5th TB, after five tanks were mired at the shoreline, proceeded towards the airfield, but after assisting in reducing enemy strongpoints, the attack was ground down by Japanese AT fire. The 3rd Battalion, the 27th Marines regimental reserve (CO Lieutenant Colonel Donn L. Robertson), landed at 1130 hours and moved up behind the 2nd Battalion, 27th Marines, to aid in neutralizing the bypassed Japanese positions. (Photo: *Pvt R. Campbell*) *(NARA)*

(**Opposite, below**) The 5th Division's reserve, the 1st Battalion, 26th Marines (CO Lieutenant Colonel Daniel C. Pollock), sets up a temporary CP soon after landing at 1500 hours on 19 February. Pollock (centre, on phone, facing camera) moved his battalion

300 yards inland from Red Beach 1 to assume frontline positions on the left of the 2nd Battalion, 27th Marines, in order to close a gap between the 27th and 28th Marines during the overnight hours. Pollock (not to be confused with 4th Division operations officer Colonel Edwin A. Pollock) would receive the Navy Cross for heroism during later combat on northern Iwo Jima. He attended West Point before enlisting in the Marine Corps in 1936, and ultimately became CO, Fleet Marine Force Pacific, in 1946. (Photo: *Cpl J. Schwartz*) (*NARA*)

(**Above**) A later wave of 5th Division riflemen and engineers disembark from their LCVP at a run at 1615 hours on 19 February. Marines burrowed into the volcanic ash for protection from Japanese artillery and mortar fire. (Photo: *Pvt G. Burns*) (YANK *magazine* / USAHEC)

(**Opposite, above**) A group of the 28th Marines, 5th Division seek cover after the 1st and 2nd Battalions landed at Green Beach on 19 February and were tasked with isolating and assaulting the strongly fortified Mount Suribachi, which USN maps codenamed HOT-ROCKS as a reference point to Mount Suribachi's highest peak. Japanese heavy artillery and mortar fire rained down from the volcano onto the Marine beachhead, especially in the 5th Division zone at Green Beach. Marine company cohesion waned as officers became casualties, compelling individual groups of Marines to advance independently to preserve the momentum. Marine 60mm mortars contributed to the forward movements of riflemen as these rounds flushed the Japanese out of their emplacements into the open, now becoming targets. By 1035 hours, a handful of Company B, 1st Battalion, 28th Marines reached Iwo's western shore, albeit with heavy casualties. (*NARA*).

(**Opposite, below**) 4th Division Marines are pinned down on one of their beaches on 19 February 1945 with an LSM (with number censored), a variety of disabled vehicles including an M4A3 tank and truck (far left), a disabled jeep (right) and abandoned LCVPs (centre and right). At 0905 hours, Colonel Walter W. Wensinger's 23rd Marines' 1st Battalion (CO Lieutenant Colonel Ralph Haas) and 2nd Battalion (CO Major Robert H. Davidson) landed abreast of one another at Yellow Beaches 1 and 2, respectively, and received only light resistance until units of the two assault battalions reached the second sand terrace, where heavy fire from two enemy blockhouses and fifty pillboxes rained down on them. By 1000 hours, LSMs brought sixteen M4A3 tanks from Company C 4th TB to the Yellow 1 and 2 Beaches. A handful of tanks were damaged by landmines or immobilized by the soft volcanic ash 150 yards from the surf. (Photo: *TSgt H.N. Gillespie*) (*NARA*)

(**Opposite, above**) 4th Division Marines advance off their landing beach with Mount Suribachi looming (background) and a Marine who perished. At noon, the 1st Battalion, 23rd Marines advanced 500 yards inland to within 200 yards of Airfield No. 1. The 2nd Battalion, 23rd Marines' forward progress was limited due to intense resistance and the lack of armoured support. Colonel Wensinger (CO, 23rd Marines) then released the regimental reserve 3rd Battalion, 23rd Marines (CO Major James S. Scales) to land along Yellow 1 Beach, advance inland, and support the 2nd Battalion, 23rd Marines with 81mm mortars in the absence of armour. Passing through beach congestion and the 1st Battalion, 23rd Marines, the 3rd Battalion, 23rd Marines incurred many casualties but reached the airfield boundary by 1700 hours. (Photo: *Associated Press photographer Joe Rosenthal*) (*NARA*)

(**Opposite, below**) Heavily kitted elements of the 4th and 5th Marines Divisions meet moving across the volcanic ash inland later on 19 February, with some wounded or dead Marines in shell holes. Airfield No. 1, D-Day's initial objective, was directly inland from the Marine assault beaches. By 1030 hours, units from eight Marine assault battalions of the 4th and 5th Divisions were ashore as M4A3 tanks of the 4th and 5th TBs began landing from the larger LSMs. (*NARA*)

(**Above**) Various amphibious landing craft are situated at the beachhead on 19 February next to a Japanese transport that was riddled by shells during the USN pre-invasion bombardment. An LVT (A)-4 (centre foreground) had a crew of four and mounted a 3-inch short-barrelled 75mm M3 howitzer in the turret of an M8 HMC tank to provide supporting fire in lieu of artillery at the beachhead. In the background are LVT 2 assault craft (background right) with either 0.50-inch calibre Browning MGs or two 20mm cannon, or both. (*NARA*)

(**Opposite, above**) A scene of carnage at the 4th Division Blue Beach 1 zone late in the day on 19 February, where the 1st and 3rd Battalions, 25th Marines, landed. Two LVT 4s are overturned, with their treads destroyed, next to a 4th TB M4A3 tank. These armoured vehicles were destroyed by either Japanese landmines planted in the volcanic ash or the ceaseless Japanese artillery and mortar bombardment of the Marine invasion beaches. The LVT 4 was an improved LVT 2 with the engine moved forward and a ramp added at the rear for easier loading and unloading, giving the LVT 4 the ability to carry cargo such as jeeps and artillery. (*NARA*)

(**Opposite, below**) Despite high surf, USCG-crewed USN LCMs and LSTs are unloaded by Marine and USN shore parties late in the day on 19 February. The beachmasters, salvage and shore parties normally kept beaches clear, but due to the intense Japanese mortar and artillery fire, the coxswains in the landing craft took the initiative to get to shore, unload and disembark from the beachhead. The anticipated good surf conditions deteriorated as the tide broke directly onto the beach, carrying small craft sideways up onto the sand. The shore became littered with supply and ammunition boxes, necessitating Marines function in a 'chain gang' capacity to get the material off the beach. Note the Marine has a Winchester Model 1912 shotgun slung across his back. (*NARA*)

(**Above**) Japanese mortar and artillery rounds plastered the Iwo Jima landing beaches on 19 February. Amtracs are ablaze and two 75mm pack howitzer positions under fire. According to Conner and Rockey, 'At the water's edge amtracs, LCMs and LCVPs were hit, burned, broached, capsized, and otherwise mangled ... the steep terraces blocked egress from the beach and extensive minefields took a heavy toll. Debris piled up everywhere. Wounded men were arriving on the beach by the dozen, where they were not much better off than they had been at the front. There was no cover to protect them and supplies of plasma and dressings ran low. The first two boats bringing in badly needed litters were blown out of the water. Casualties were being hit a second time as they lay helpless, under blankets, awaiting evacuation to ships.' (*NARA*)

A battered LCI with a dead 40mm Bofors AA gun crewman at his post and a wounded sailor. On 17 February, two days pre-invasion, LCI gunboats and rocket ships moved close to the shoreline to cover USN frogmen clearing the beach approaches and checking surf conditions. At 1100 hours, the Japanese, believing this was the actual invasion, opened fire with their heaviest artillery. The USN suffered 170 casualties but the frogmen returned with knowledge of the beach and surf conditions. (*NARA*)

Two DUKWs swamped with water sit at the shoreline with a disabled jeep and LCVP (far right) on 19 February. Marines, USN 'Seabees', and USCG landing parties formed lines to offload any salvageable supplies from the DUKWs. The DUKW was designed by General Motors Corporation (GMC) engineers in 1942 and manufactured quickly by converting a GMC 2.5-ton truck into an oceangoing vessel capable of contributing to amphibious warfare. GMC produced 21,147 DUKWs from 1942 to 1945. The DUKW could carry 2.5 tons maximally before structural and navigable ability suffered in most conditions. At Iwo Jima, DUKW operators manoeuvred in the water amid Japanese gunfire while they carried 105mm howitzers, Marines and ammunition to the shore. The rough surf on 19 February contributed to these two DUKWs becoming deluged with seawater. (*NARA*)

A Marine M4A2 or M4A3 comes ashore from a landing ship's bow ramp onto Iwo Jima's volcanic ash with its wading exhaust visible with fumes. The 4th and 5th TBs had the heavier M4A3 tanks, including four in each battalion, each equipped with the modified USN Mk 1 flamethrower replacing the 75mm turret gun. The 3rd Battalion still employed M4A2 tanks, arriving on Iwo on 23 February. A major difference between the M4A2 and M4A3 in the Pacific was that the former used diesel as its fuel while the latter was gasoline powered. (Photo: *Cpl A. Genco*) (NARA)

A disabled M4A3 tank with its tread thrown from a landmine just inland from the invasion beach with the USN armada (background). A dead Japanese soldier lies next to a dirt path that the tank attempted to traverse. On 19 February, the 1st Battalion, 23rd Marines, 4th Division fought through intense Japanese gunfire and artillery, and despite incurring many casualties was 500 yards inland at 1200 hours, just 200 yards short of Airfield No. 1. Supported by tanks, the battalion's left flank reached the airfield at 1405 hours, but intense AT fire caused the Marines and M4A3 tanks to withdraw behind a depressed edge of the field. (Photo: *SSgt M. Kauffman*) (*NARA*)

(**Above**) 5th Division Marines take cover as an M4A3 tank advances towards enemy forti-fications near Airfield No. 1 on 19 February. It was during the fight to reach this airfield that Medal of Honor recipient Gunnery Sergeant John Basilone was killed by a Japanese mortar shell. (Photo: *Cpl J. Schwartz*) (*NARA*)

(**Opposite, above**) Two 5th Marine Division replacements at the beachhead ponder their upcoming inland movements with Mount Suribachi looming. The replacements were not only new to combat but were also unknown to their assigned unit. Replacement losses within the first forty-eight hours of combat were appalling, yet those that survived formed cohesive bonds with the campaign's veterans. (Photo: *WO O. Newcomb*) (*NARA*)

(**Opposite, below**) A 2nd Battalion, 24th Marines, 4th Division unit, situated 500 yards inland from Yellow Beach 2, awaits orders to attack on Airfield No. 1 at 0900 hours on 20 February. Major General Cates ordered ashore the 1st and 2nd Battalions of Colonel Walter I. Jordan's 24th Marines, the division reserve, at 1405 hours on 19 February to be attached to the hard-pressed 25th and 23rd Marines. The 2nd Battalion, 24th Marines (CO Lieutenant Colonel Richard Rothwell) landed at 1650 hours and rapidly moved inland to relieve the 2nd Battalion, 23rd Marines by 1800 hours. They dug in for the night defence just short of the airfield and withstood Japanese mortar and artillery fire during the overnight hours. (Photo: *Sgt N. Ragus*) (*NARA*)

(**Above**) A Marine BAR gunner moves uphill with other members of the 26th Marines, 5th Division to the west of Airfield No. 1 on 21 February. The M1918A2 BAR, heavy at 19lb, provided sustained semi-automatic fire support to a Marine assault squad with its twenty-round trapezoidal-shaped magazine of 0.30-inch calibre cartridges and was especially useful against Japanese trying to escape from concealment after being flushed out by grenades or flame. (Photo: *Cpl J. Schwartz*) (*NARA*)

(**Opposite, above**) A 5th Division Marine carrying his M1 semi-automatic carbine rifle crouches as he climbs a ridge under Japanese machine-gun fire through thick, sparse brush near Airfield No. 1 on 20 February. (Photo: *Sgt J.T. Dreyfuss*) (*NARA*)

(**Opposite, below**) A Japanese MG emplacement near Airfield No.1, which stalled the initial advance of the 23rd Marines, 4th Division in the seizure of that major objective late in the day of 19 February. Japanese fortifications at Airfield No. 1, which included AA guns and small-calibre artillery, necessitated the regimental reserve, the 3rd Battalion, 23rd Marines (CO Major James S. Scales) to land along Yellow Beach later on D-Day and move 200 yards inland to support the 2nd Battalion, 23rd Marines. Once ashore, the 3rd Battalion, 23rd Marines began to take shelling and gunfire, but reached the near edges of the airfield by 1700 hours. (*NARA*)

(**Above**) A dead Japanese soldier lies near his Arisaka rifle serving as a marker near Airfield No. 1 soon after its capture on 20 February. On that day, at 1630 hours, elements of the 23rd Marines seized positions along the western edge of Airfield No. 1 in order to make contact with the 27th Marines, 5th Division on the left by 1800 hours. Heavy casualties throughout 20 February further reduced the combat efficiency of Cates's 4th Division, but the capture of Airfield No. 1 was completed. (Photo: *Sgt N. Ragus*) (*NARA*)

(**Opposite, above**) Weary 4th Division assault troops of Company G, 2nd Battalion, 24th Marines rest in a ditch near a previous Japanese shelter (left background) while waiting for M4A3 tanks to move forward to blast the numerous pillboxes and gun emplacements between Airfields Nos. 1 and 2 on 22 February. (Photo: *Sgt N. Ragus*) (*NARA*)

(**Opposite, below**) AN IJA Type 4 20mm twin-mounted AA gun was destroyed by a Marine M4A3 tank at the edge of Airfield No. 1. The Japanese gun was situated within an open concrete block casemate with covered areas to the right side for ammunition stowage, as dead Japanese gunners lay under and to the left of the twin barrels. (*NARA*)

(**Opposite, above**) With the USN landing fleet in the background, wrecks of Japanese planes destroyed during the island's naval and aerial bombardment are situated at the very eastern edge of Airfield No. 1. This view demonstrates the terraced terrain that Marine infantry and armour had to ascend from the shoreline to reach the airfield. (*NARA*)

(**Opposite, below**) Marines work past burned and wrecked Japanese aircraft at Airfield No. 1. Landmines, 'booby traps', in addition to snipers, had to be removed by Marine engineers and USN 'Seabees'. (*NARA*)

(**Above**) Marine riflemen fire on Japanese snipers lurking in wrecked aircraft at Airfield No. 1 soon after its capture on 20 February. Often, tank dozers, armoured bulldozers, or tank flamethrowers were employed to ultimately clear the area of airplane wrecks and lurking snipers for the restoration work to begin to make the airfield operational. (Photo: *WO O. Newcomb*) (*NARA*)

(**Above**) Marines standing in shell holes at Airfield No. 1 observe an M4A3 tank engage surviving Japanese snipers still lurking in destroyed enemy aircraft on 21 February. On 20 February at 2200 hours, the Japanese attacked the 27th Marines, 5th Division in company strength just west of Airfield No. 1. Waiting until the Japanese were almost on top of their positions, Marines responded with machine-gun and rifle fire as flares caught the enemy in bright light who succumbed to a barrage of 5th Division howitzer fire from the base of Mount Suribachi. Along the northern edge of the airfield, the 25th Marines, 4th Division were attacked at dawn on 21 February as Japanese infiltrators moved between rocks and ravines to attempt surprise on the Marine line. Nearly a hundred enemy bodies were counted at daylight, killed by Marine infantry and artillery. (*NARA*)

(**Opposite, above**) At 1035 hours on 26 February, two Marine Stinson OY single-engine observation planes ('Grasshoppers') of Marine Observation Squadron (VMO)-4 flew in from the escort carrier USS *Wake Island* to become the first aircraft to land on Airstrip No. 1. Marine pilot Lieutenant H. Olson taxis down a runway with a 3rd Division Marine hanging onto a strut to guide the plane as the airstrip was under fire and cratered from shelling. These initial two observation planes were followed the next day by (VMO)-5. The contributions of the pilots and aerial spotters from three Marine Observation Squadrons (VMOs-1, -4 and -5) provided important intelligence in spotting enemy artillery and mortar positions and then reporting them back to fire control centres. These observation planes initially flew from escort carriers or were launched from LST 776, but eventually took off from the captured airstrips. All these squadrons' planes received heavy Japanese AA fire, not only while airborne but also while being serviced on the airstrips. Japanese AA gunners did shoot down some of the 'Grasshoppers', which flew approximately 600 missions with the three VMO squadrons in support of the three Marine divisions. (Photo: *Pfc R.R. Dodds*) (*NARA*)

(**Below**) The first carrier plane takes off from now operational Airfield No. 1 after the aircraft was repaired on Iwo Jima following a forced landing on 28 February. USN fighter-bombers flying from escort carriers, after Spruance's fleet carriers departed, were critical for ground support of advancing Marines. (*NARA*)

68013

(**Opposite, above**) A USAAF 7th Fighter Command North American P-51 Mustang fighter-bomber returns to land at Airfield No. 1 on 11 March after a combat sortie from Iwo Jima over Chuichi Jima and Haha Jima in the Bonin Islands. On 6 March, the 15th Fighter Group of 7th Fighter Command first flew into Iwo Jima. This group included the 47th Fighter Squadron, which was to serve initially as the fighter escort for the B-29s over Tokyo. As for direct fighter support for the Marines on the ground, the P-51s could deliver 1,000lb bombs with twelve-second delay fuses that could blow the sides of the entire cliffs into the ocean off the west coast of the island, exposing caves and tunnels for direct gunfire by USN warships. With the addition of the 47th Fighter Squadron, the USN escort carriers were able to depart the area. (*NARA*)

(**Opposite, below**) A North American P-51 Mustang readies for take-off on their first escort mission on 7 April from one of the two operational Iwo Jima airfields, this one improved with Marston matting. The Mustangs provided fighter escort for the Mariana-based B-29 Superfortresses as they had the requisite range (with auxiliary wing fuel tanks) to accompany the B-29s to Tokyo and other Home Island targets and back to Iwo Jima. The Mustangs flew at the performance limit during the round trip to Japan, using a B-29 as a navigation aircraft for the long flights over water. Iwo Jima's captured and improved airfields provided emergency landing fields for crippled or low-on-fuel B-29s on their return flight to their Mariana Islands bases, enabling them to avoid crashing into the Pacific. (*NARA*)

(**Above**) A B-29 Superfortress is shown after it ditched in the ocean offshore as Airfield No. 1 was non-operational due to fog. All of the B-29's crewmembers were able to swim to shore safely. (*NARA*)

Other Marine aviation units contributed significantly to Iwo Jima's capture. Shown are two Grumman TBFs of the 4th Marine Air Wing (MAW) on Airfield No. 2, which attacked IJN ships trying to resupply Iwo Jima from other bases in the Volcano and Bonin Islands. These interdiction raids, combined with USN submarine attacks on enemy shipping, significantly reduced munitions and barbed wire deliveries to Kuribayashi's troops. A four-engine B-24 Liberator is shown (right background). *(NARA)*

Chapter Five

Securing the Island

Mount Suribachi

Mount Suribachi's capture was tasked to the 28th Marines, 5th Division, which began its assault at 0830 hours on 20 February against 1,600 isolated suicidal Japanese in hundreds of pillboxes, caves with interconnecting tunnels, blockhouses and dugouts at the volcano's base, but advanced only 70 yards. The remainder of the 5th Division and the entire 4th Division were capturing Airfield No. 1 and then preparing to assault Airfield No. 2 before advancing into Iwo Jima's heavily fortified Motoyama Plateau and northern sector.

During the morning of 21 February, American air sorties bombed and strafed enemy positions 100 yards in front of the 28th Marines' lines, and with effective M4A3 tank use, gains of 500 to 1,000 yards among the three battalions were made. The next morning, 22 February, after a night of Japanese infiltrations, the 28th Marines advanced without air support due to their proximity to the volcano and the inclement weather, but accompanied by 5th TB M4A3 tanks. Overcoming enemy mortar and small arms fire, the 28th Marines by 1630 hours surrounded Mount Suribachi, although there were still a few hundred Japanese concealed within the volcano's caves.

On 21 February, the 23rd and 25th Marines, 4th Division continued their slow advance along the eastern side of the island. The progress made by the 23rd Marines only amounted to 100 yards before digging in for the night at 1800 hours. The 25th Marines with tank and artillery support drove the Japanese from the elevated terrain around 'The Quarry' and the nearby cliffs, progressing 300 yards along the shore of the East Boat Basin, albeit with heavy casualties, including Lieutenant Colonel Hollis U. Mustain, CO 1st Battalion, 25th Marines, who was KIA at the front lines, with battalion leadership turned over to his XO, Major Fenton J. Mee.

The 21st Marines, 3rd Division, commanded by Colonel Hartnoll Withers, landed on 21 February, preparing to relieve the 23rd Marines, 4th Division the next day at 0500 hours. Japanese gunfire from interlocking pillboxes and bunkers in the taxiways and on the high ground between the two airfields delayed these newly arrived 3rd Division Marines from relieving the 23rd Marines for six hours. On 22 February, VAC front lines were still 1,200 yards short of the 0-1 Line, which bisected the north–south runway of Airfield No 2; however, the 28th Marines' flag raisings on Mount Suribachi's summit occurred the next day, 23 February (see Chapter 6).

Advance on Airfield No. 2

VAC operations after 24 February were for a three-Marine division northern advance, with the 5th Division along Iwo Jima's west coast, the 3rd Division (less the still afloat 3rd Marines as VAC reserve) in the centre, and the 4th Division on the island's east coast. Marine M4A3s were damaged or destroyed by mines and artillery, with infantry units receiving intense fire on Airfield No. 2 runways. Initially, the 2nd and 3rd Battalions, 24th Marines advancing alongside the 21st Marines towards Airfield No. 2 made good progress, with the 2nd Battalion, 24th Marines reaching the eastern end of the east–west runway by 1100 hours. Then, the 24th Marines approached the core of General Kuribayashi's central Iwo defences, which incorporated commanding terrain features rising to the north. After making gains, the 2nd and 3rd Battalions, 24th Marines received a tremendous Japanese mortar barrage at 1600 hours, which wounded Lieutenant Colonel Alexander A. Vandegrift, Jr., the 3rd Battalion CO and son of the Marine Corps Commandant and Guadalcanal legend, in both legs, necessitating his evacuation. The 1st Battalion, 24th Marines also attacked but its advance was impeded by rough and concealed Japanese emplacements and caves. The eastern portion of Airfield No. 2 and 'Charlie-Dog Ridge' (named after its map grid square location) were secured at heavy cost on 24 February. The next day, small groups of Marines accompanied by tanks managed to make it across Airfield No. 2's runway.

The Drive to the North of Iwo Jima

The 0-2 Phase Line stretched from the island's west coast and moved south of Nishi and the incomplete Airfield No. 3. Then, the line moved north of Motoyama Village, passing to the eastern shore at Tachiiwa Point. There were three hills with an elevation of 362 feet, designated as A, B and C. Hill 362-A was located in north-western Iwo in Rockey's 5th Division sector. Hill 362-B, also in the 5th Division sector, was situated in the north-central portion of the island. Hill 362-C, located to the north-east, was in the 3rd Division zone.

To the east, the 4th Division attacked obstacles such as Hill 382 – the highest elevation on northern Iwo, just east of Airfield No. 2, pockmarked with countless pillboxes and caves. A semi-circular shallow depression 400 yards to the south-east, dubbed the 'Amphitheatre', had strongly constructed defences and a nearby craggy ridge surmounted by a massive concrete communications blockhouse, which withstood days of flamethrower and tank gunfire, called 'Turkey Knob', immediately to the east. Another obstacle was the village of Minami, now a rubble heap from naval bombardment, but studded with MG positions. This Japanese defensive complex area located east of Airfield No. 2 became known to the 4th Division as the 'Meatgrinder'.

Early on 25 February, the 4th Division's 23rd and 24th Marines and the attached 21st Marines, 3rd Division attacked this 'Meatgrinder' area defended by Major General Sadasue Senda and his 2nd IMB, consisting of five infantry battalions, both artillery and engineer battalions, and a field hospital. Senda's defences also included the men and concealed tanks of Baron Nishi's 26th Tank Regiment. At the end of the day, only 100 yards were gained, at a cost of 500 Marine casualties.

The 4th Division finally seized Hill 382, with heavy casualties, in early March. The salient comprised of the 'Amphitheatre', the ruins of Minami Village and 'Turkey Knob' were to hold out until 15 March and be the scene of some of the bloodiest actions of the entire campaign.

The 5th Division attacked Nishi Ridge, and Hills 362-A and 362-B. On 2 March, the 26th Marines, 5th Division mounted a successful, albeit bloody, attack to finally seize Hill 362-B. The day-long struggle accounted for 500 Marine casualties. The 3rd Division assaulted the heavily fortified area to the north of Airfield No. 2 and Hills 199 OBOE and PETER, taking three days of intense combat to secure before contesting Hill 362-C, south-east of the incomplete Airfield No. 3.

During the initial nine days of VAC's northern drive there was a net gain of 4,000 yards at an enormous cost of 7,000 Marine casualties to capture Airfield No. 2, Hill 382 and Hills 362-A and 362-B. By 6 March, the terrain, from an assault perspective, deteriorated into narrow, winding ravines with lingering sulphur fumes that became rock-strewn killing zones. On this day, a 9th and 21st Marines, 3rd Division assault was stopped after only 200 yards were gained despite the heavy expenditure of 155mm, 105mm and 75mm artillery rounds along with 50 15-inch and 400 8-inch shells fired at the dug-in enemy by battleships and cruisers respectively. On 7 March, another 3rd Division assault commenced against Hill 362-C, which was finally captured by the 3rd Battalion, 9th Marines (CO Lieutenant Colonel Harold C. Boehm). The next day, 8 March, the 9th Marines advanced 400 yards beyond Hill 362-C towards the sea, with a USN destroyer firing into the draws that led down to the water, enabling Erskine's 3rd Division's two Marine regiments to reach the water's edge on the evening of 9 March, achieving its primary mission to break through and hold 800 yards of Iwo's north-eastern shore. This accomplishment bisected the shrinking redoubt still in Japanese hands with Lieutenant General Kuribayashi and the remnants of his garrison near Kitano Point to an area of one square mile.

By 16 March, Cates's 4th Division moved over hills along the east and seized the coast road. Many Japanese strongpoints were engaged and destroyed from the rear as almost all of Iwo Jima was in Marine possession. After Hill 362's capture, the 3rd Division continued its attacks on Kuribayashi's redoubt, isolating them into smaller pockets of resistance, which managed to hold out until 21 March, an entire week after the island was declared secure. Three days later, Kuribayashi's command bunker near Kitano Point was taken by Marine artillery and flamethrowers.

Even Tokyo announced on radio the fall of Iwo Jima, but fighting continued despite another American flag raising on 14 March (after twenty-four days of bitter combat) to signify the occupation of the island. The official end of the campaign would not be until 26 March, when the 5th Division squeezed the

Japanese during fighting in 'The Gorge' into a final pocket eliminated by units of the 26th and 28th Marines on 25 March.

Only 216 Japanese POWs were taken from a garrison of more than 20,000 in the thirty-six-day campaign for the island. The US Army's 147th Infantry Regiment ('Cavemen') killed 1,602 Japanese and captured 867 more in the initial two months after the Marines left.

5th TB M4A3 tanks assist 28th Marines assaulting Mount Suribachi's base at 0825 hours on 21 February. The 2nd Battalion, 28th Marines advanced along the eastern shore and met enemy rifle and machine-gun fire followed by a curtain of mortar rounds. By 1100 hours, some infantry gains were made only after tanks, 75mm and 105mm howitzers, 37mm AT guns, and unarmoured rocket truck detachments bombarded Japanese positions. At 1200 hours, 1st Battalion, 28th Marines was positioned at Mount Suribachi's western base. Two hours later, the 3rd Battalion reached the centre of Mount Suribachi's base after repelling a Japanese counterattack. White smoke rose from caves after Marine flamethrowers' assaults. Fortunately, direct USN naval and aerial bombardment disabled many of Colonel Kanehiko Atsuchi's (CO Mount Suribachi sector) large-calibre guns on 16–19 February. However, Atsuchi commanded a garrison of 2,000 soldiers and sailors firing their small-calibre ordnance from excavated caves honeycombing the dormant volcano, also containing pillboxes, OPs and tunnels. Some of the strongest Japanese defences, including camouflaged concrete blockhouses, existed at Suribachi's rock-strewn base and within the initial 100 feet up the slopes. Lieutenant General Kuribayashi planned the Suribachi defences to hold out for 10–14 days. By the evening of 21 February, the three battalions of Colonel Liversedge's 28th Marines formed a semicircle surrounding the volcano. (Photo: *Pfc A.L. Farnum*) (NARA)

Japanese machine gunners and snipers within pillboxes amid scrubwood at Mount Suribachi's base required 28th Marines' demolition and flamethrower teams to reduce them on 22 February, since heavier ordnance, such as 105mm howitzers of the 5th Division's 13th Marines (Artillery) and USN airstrikes were often fruitless against these concealed concrete-reinforced positions. (Photo: *Pvt G. Burns*) (YANK *magazine / USAHEC*)

(**Above**) A patrol of the 28th Marines, 5th Division moves through scrubwood and dense undergrowth at Mount Suribachi's base on 22 February. The Marines in the patrol's rear carry a sound system's components, which once set up, was to lure Japanese soldiers out of the numerous caves on Mount Suribachi to surrender, which very few did. (Photo: *Sgt L.R. Burmeister*) (*NARA*)

(**Opposite, above**) A 28th Marines patrol moves around a disabled Japanese 120mm CD gun emplaced in a rock and concrete casemate carved into the face of Mount Suribachi's slope, on 21 February. Many of these larger-calibre guns were neutralized by pre-invasion naval and aerial bombardment. The Mount Suribachi Sector commander, Colonel Kanehiko Atsuchi, and Major Nagahiko Matsushita, CO 10th Independent AT Battalion, were faced with mounting casualties during the Marine advance on the volcano. Ultimately, with telephone lines destroyed, the Japanese used flares at night to request northern sector artillery and mortar support. After securing Mount Suribachi's summit on 23 February, the 28th Marines spent days sealing caves and mopping up stubborn Japanese defenders. Most caves on Mount Suribachi had multiple entrances and different exits as well as many levels. (*NARA*)

(**Opposite, below**) A 28th Marines regimental CP that was wiped out at 0800 hours on 22 February by a direct Japanese mortar round, killing regimental surgeon USN Lieutenant Commander Daniel J. McCarthy, is now reoccupied by another group of Marines forming a small-unit CP. The Marine standing in the centre holds a 5lb Signal Corps Radio (SCR) 536, commonly called a 'walkie-talkie'. The crevice-like terrain with surrounding rocks provided protection against Japanese artillery, but it was not impervious to enemy mortar rounds and grenades. (*NARA*)

(**Above**) A 28th Marines rifleman covers the left flank of a reinforced forty-man Marine platoon as it neared Mount Suribachi's crater rim on the morning of 23 February. The patrol's nucleus was comprised of twenty-five Marines of the 3rd Platoon, Company E, 2nd Battalion, dispatched by the battalion CO, Lieutenant Colonel Chandler Johnson. It was led by 1st Lieutenant Harold G. Schrier (Co E XO), who was given a folded American flag that had been brought ashore by the 2nd Battalion's adjutant, 1st Lieutenant George G. Wells. The patrol reached the crater's rim thirty minutes after leaving Johnson's primitive 2nd Battalion CP at the volcano's base, noting a few battered gun emplacements and some cave entrances but no living Japanese. Suribachi loomed over and threatened Marine assault beaches and landing craft, causing many casualties until the volcano with its guns was captured. (Photo: *SSgt L. Lowery*) (Leatherneck *magazine / NARA*)

(**Opposite**) A line of M4A2 tanks of the 3rd TB, 3rd Division moves between Airfields Nos. 1 and 2 on 25 February. At 0910 hours on 24 February, VAC resumed its northern Iwo drive with the 26th Marines, 5th Division on the left, the 21st Marines, 3rd Division in the centre, and the 24th Marines, 4th Division on the right. The TBs of the three Marine divisions (under the command of Lieutenant Colonel William R. Collins) were of paramount importance to successfully advance on Airfield No. 2. Previously, on 22 February, the Marine 4th TB had nineteen M4A3s disabled, leaving only twenty-eight operational.

On 24 February, thirty-four M4A3s of the 5th TB spearheaded the armoured thrust, with seventeen put out of commission by horned mines and buried aerial bombs detonating as contact torpedoes as well as by accurate Japanese AT gunfire. Marine engineers cleared a lane from mines in order for a dozen tanks to resume an advance and reach Airfield No. 2's edges via an eastern taxiway, which commenced firing on Japanese positions to the airfield's north. The tanks accompanied the three battalions of the 26th Marines advancing abreast of one another. On 24 February, the 21st Marines attacked without armoured support and despite high casualties, including officers, elements of this regiment crossed the airfield and reduced interconnected enemy pillboxes, trenches and AT gun positions, commanded by Japanese Colonel Masuo Ikeda, on elevated ground to the north of the two runways' junction before Japanese artillery halted the advance of the 3rd Battalion, 21st Marines at 1200 hours. After a combined naval and aerial bombardment at 1330 hours, the 26th and 21st Marines renewed their assault with tank support attacking the high ground north of the airfield. Marine M4A3s were able to operate from the western end of both runways and fired on Japanese gun emplacements and pillboxes, with the 21st Marines units holding on to their gains. By 1600 hours, the 3rd Battalion, 26th Marines advanced 400 yards beyond the 21st Marines' forward positions. (Photo: *TSgt J. Heiberger*) (NARA)

(**Opposite, above**) A platoon leader in Company L, 3rd Battalion, 21st Marines, 3rd Division moves forward on 24 February, attempting to seize Airfield No. 2. On 20 February, due to strong Japanese resistance, the battle-tested 21st Marines, 3rd Division, still on transports as VAC reserve, boarded assault craft when surf and beach congestion improved. Once ashore on 21 February, the 21st Marines, 3rd Division were temporarily placed under Cates's 4th Division command. (Photo: *Cpl W.G Page*) (NARA)

(**Opposite, below**) Marines from the HQ Company, 3rd Battalion, 21st Marines, 3rd Division fire their 81mm mortar at Japanese positions on Airfield No. 2's north end on 24 February after a tremendous naval bombardment of the airfield. The attack against Airfield No. 2 was against runways sown with mines and covered by direct fire from artillery and revetted tanks. The 3rd Battalion, 21st Marines charged across Airfield No. 2 and uphill against well-defended belts of interconnected pillboxes, trenches, tunnels and AT positions comprising some of Kuribayashi's main defensive belts. After hand-to-hand combat with IJA Colonel Ikeda's troops, it appeared that the position was secured but Japanese artillery hit the forwardmost elements of the 3rd Battalion, 21st Marines, stopping its advance. The drive to Airfield No. 2 this day was horrific, with gains of only 200–1,000 yards at an enormous cost of 773 Marines KIA and 3,741 WIA, of which, 300 would subsequently perish from their wounds. Cates's 4th Division's combat efficiency was reduced to 60 per cent. The 5th Division suffered 3,000 casualties, with the 26th Marines losing 21 officers and 332 enlisted men. (Photo: *SSgt J.F. Galloway*) (NARA)

(**Above**) 27th Marines, 5th Division, with their MG carts, take cover on a road paralleling Airfield No. 2 under Japanese mortar and sniper fire on 24 February. Similarly, the movements of the 4th Division with Colonel Withers' attached 21st Marines, 3rd Division against the Airfield No. 2 were repelled by Japanese 47mm AT guns, mutually supportive blockhouses and pillboxes with tunnels, and landmines. The 21st Marines consolidated their positions for the night at the southern edge of the airfield after incurring heavy casualties with limited ground gained. The 24th Marines, 4th Division, under Colonel Walter I. Jordan, advanced 300 yards after difficult fighting on broken terrain on 24 February, and dug in at 1500 hours as their flank was insecure as the right side of the VAC's advance on Airfield No. 2. (Photo: *Sgt D.G. Christian*) (NARA)

(**Above**) A Japanese SNLF soldier (referred to as a marine by some) was killed by Company F, 2nd Battalion, 21st Marines, 3rd Division near Airfield No. 2. The 21st Marines, 3rd Division during the early afternoon of 28 February, following a second massive artillery barrage against stiffened Japanese resistance, stormed into the destroyed Motoyama Village, the largest settlement on Iwo Jima. Japanese MG troops and snipers were occupying the ruins and were evicted by the regiment's 3rd Battalion (CO Lieutenant Colonel Wendell H. Duplantis) as the Marines occupied the heights overlooking the eastern end of the unfinished Airfield No. 3. (Photo: *Sgt D.G. Christian*) (*NARA*)

(**Opposite, above**) On 26 February, the 28th Marines, 5th Division (CO Colonel Harry Liversedge) with tank support frontally attacked Hill 362-A, 600 yards south-east of Nishi Village and west of Motoyama Village, in rocky northern Iwo Jima. The explosions seen are Japanese mortar rounds landing near a 5th TB M4A3 tank. The attack gained only 30 yards, with thirty Marine casualties incurred as this Japanese defensive locale was surrounded by pillboxes and caves. The 5th TB's M4A3 tanks, moving through the rocks and boulders to give infantry support, were ineffective against the enemy's impregnable complex of defences. Elsewhere, on 27 February, other 5th TB M4A3 tanks smashed through the Japanese defences to a depth of 100 yards and the 27th Marines, 5th Division (CO Colonel Thomas A. Wornham) advanced up the west coast assisted by naval gunfire offshore. (Photo: *Pfc C. Jones*) (*NARA*)

(**Opposite, below**) A Marine hurls a hand grenade (right) at a Japanese position as two others provide covering fire in close-action combat in northern Iwo Jima's rocky terrain. On 27 February, the 1st and 2nd Battalions, 9th Marines (COs Lieutenant Colonel Carey Randal and Lieutenant Colonel Robert Cushman, respectively) advanced on Hill PETER and the slopes of Hill 199 OBOE, 250 yards to the north-east. Three hours later, a platoon from the 1st Battalion reached the summit of Hill PETER but became isolated by

murderous gunfire from enemy strongpoints atop Hill 199 OBOE. Two hours of chaotic fighting ensued as Marine Private Wilson D. Watson, a BAR gunner, charged an enemy pillbox MG atop Hill 199 OBOE, firing his automatic rifle and killing the occupants by throwing two hand grenades through the emplacement's opening. Watson then went after other Japanese positions on Hill 199 OBOE, wiping them out single-handedly and killing over eighty enemy soldiers. Watson was awarded a Congressional Medal of Honor for his solitary display of heroism. (*NARA*)

(**Above**) 3rd Division Marines fire their M1 Garand semi-automatic rifle (right) and M1 semi-automatic carbine (left) from a shell hole amid the ruins of Motoyama Village on 28 February. The sulphur mine and refinery ruins situated just to the village's west are behind the Marines. (Photo: *Sgt R. Cooke*) (NARA)

(**Opposite, above**) On 28 February, two 27th Marines, 5th Division carry ammunition boxes on Hill 362-A, west of Motoyama Village and the incomplete Airfield No. 3, and south-east of Nishi Village. At 0900 hours on 1 March, the 28th Marines with the 5th TB and the attached 3rd Battalion, 27th Marines, continued the Hill 362-A attack as the 1st and 2nd Battalions, 28th Marines reached the ridge's top ninety minutes later. There, they discovered a steep drop of 100 feet into a rocky draw, which levelled for 200 yards before rising again sharply to form Nishi Ridge. Twenty Marines from Company B, 1st Battalion, 28th Marines were sent to clear the ridge of snipers but only seven returned. Even with the support of tanks, the 1st and 2nd Battalions, 28th Marines were stalled for the remainder of 1 March along the crest and at the base of Hill 362-A, where the Japanese held out in caves. However, the 3rd Battalion, 28th Marines gained 350 yards near the west coast before halting the advance due to the stalling of the other two regimental battalions. By the end of 1 March, Hill 362-A and a rocky ridgeline extending to the west coast was captured at the cost of 224 Marine casualties. The next day, 2 March, a Japanese high-velocity shell killed Lieutenant Colonel Chandler Johnson, the 2nd Battalion CO, as he inspected the front lines, one week after his troops reached Mount Suribachi's summit and raised the two flags. By evening, the battle of Hill 362-A was over. The 5th Division attacked Nishi Ridge and Hill 362-B on 3 March. (Photo: *Pvt R. Campbell*) (NARA)

(**Below**) Two 26th Marines (CO Colonel Chester B. Graham), 5th Division provide covering fire for a smoking 5th TB M4A3 disabled by a Japanese shell during the advance on Nishi Village on 2 March. The 5th Division engineers were of paramount importance in clearing the approaches to the enemy pillboxes and fortifications that were mined. The 26th Marines made the biggest advance, 500 yards, that day. (Photo: *Cpl E. Jones*) (*NARA*)

(**Above**) A 5th Division Marine (right) rises from a rocky shell hole shared with two other Marines to fire his M1 semi-automatic carbine at Japanese snipers during the northern advance on 11 March, in terrain characteristic of northern Iwo Jima. In the two weeks spanning 25 February to 10 March, the 5th Division drove 3,000 yards up Iwo Jima's western coast from Airfield No. 2 to a line that stretched across the narrow northern end of the island. To the 5th Division's north, Kuribayashi repositioned his final IJA 109th Division HQ within a rocky redoubt of less than one square mile with troops of the 2nd Battalion, 145th Infantry Regiment, and the remnants of the 3rd Battalion, 17th Independent Mixed Regiment. (Photo: *Sgt J.T. Dreyfuss*) (NARA)

(**Opposite, above**) A Japanese soldier lies dead with a grenade in the palm of his left hand at Mount Suribachi's base on 23 February. Japanese infiltrators leaving their cover and camouflage to attack with grenades were not uncommon. On 21 February, Sergeant Henry Hansen of the 3rd Platoon, Company E, 2nd Battalion, 28th Marines, 5th Division, who would help raise the first flag on the volcano two days later, was within a few yards of Mount Suribachi's base when a camouflaged bunker was spotted. Hansen dived for cover after seeing a hand grenade thrown at them. Private 1st Class Donald J. Ruhl, another platoon member, dived on the grenade as it detonated, taking the full impact and dying while saving his sergeant's life. Ruhl was awarded a posthumous Congressional Medal of Honor. (Photo: *Pvt R. Campbell*) (NARA)

(**Below**) Marines take cover within northern Iwo's rock crevices and gaze at smoke billowing nearby. Late in the northern Iwo campaign, the 5th Marine Division cornered the last Japanese defenders in 'The Gorge', where the 5th TB's M4A3 'Zippo Tanks' expended napalm-thickened fuel at the rate of 10,000 gallons per day. The division's after-action report stated that the M4A3 flamethrower tank was the one weapon that caused the Japanese defenders to leave their caves and rock crevices and run out in the open for Marine riflemen to gun them down. (Photo: *TSgt H.N. Gillespie*) *(NARA)*

A 4th Division platoon sergeant leads his men from a tank disabled on a crushed Japanese pillbox during combat in the 'Meatgrinder' sector on 1 March. Nearly 500 men were lost on 25 February, the first day in the 'Meatgrinder', for a gain of 100 yards. During the attack on Hill 382, tanks could not operate on the rocky hillside and it was also impossible to bring up flamethrowers and Marine demolition engineers, as Kuribayashi mastered the terrain to his advantage. Major General Senda, CO 2nd Mixed Brigade, maintained Kuribayashi's camouflage discipline with the exception of 8 March, when after days of constant pressure in a shrinking defence area he launched a full-scale counterattack, hitting Company E, 2nd Battalion, 23rd Marines. This raged throughout the overnight hours and expended 500 grenades, 200 60mm HE mortar shells and an uncounted quantity of 0.30-inch calibre ammunition for MGs and rifles. Other units of the 23rd and 24th Marines also participated to repel the counterattack. By daylight, 800 Japanese bodies were counted as the 23rd and 24th Marines incurred 90 KIA and 257 WIA. (Photo: *Sgt L.R. Burmeister*) (*NARA*)

Several caves that were excavated before the invasion are visible on a hill within the 3rd Marine Division sector on 4 March. One of Kuribayashi's first decisions at the end of July 1944 was expediting the tunnel and cave construction in addition to fortifying the many natural caves. The island's soft stone enabled easier digging and volcanic ash was used to reinforce the structures. Cave specialists from Japan arrived to design these fortifications and to insure good ventilation as cave entrances and exits were built at different levels. In addition, tunnels within the caves were laid out to neutralize the anticipated blasts of bombardment and Marine artillery. On 28 February, 6,000 Marines of the 4th Division mounted another assault on Hill 382 and 'Turkey Knob' in the 'Meatgrinder' sector. Tanks were of little help against these fortifications because they could not manoeuvre in this terrain or overcome landmines. Also, the 75mm turret gun of the M4A3 could not penetrate the concrete-reinforced walls of the large communication centre atop 'Turkey Knob'. Colonel Edwin A. Pollock, 4th Division operations officer, surmised that despite only small Marine gains, Cates's division had slaughtered hundreds of Japanese troops every day in the 'Meatgrinder' as the central core of resistance before Hill 382 and 'Turkey Knob' were beginning to crack. (*NARA*)

A 28th Marine (right) hurls a grenade in a duel with the Japanese cave occupants during the Nishi Ridge assault on 3 March get to Hill 362-B. A 5th Division Marine lies dead (far right). Two days earlier, the 28th Marines 1st and 2nd Battalions attacked Hill 362-A against moderate resistance. By mid-morning of 1 March, Liversedge's regiment, veterans of their previous Mount Suribachi assault, pushed to Hill 362-A's crest. However, most of the Japanese defenders escaped through the hill's network of tunnels to take up new positions on Nishi Ridge, the same elevation as Hill 362-A, located 300 yards to the west. Nishi Ridge bristled with excavated fortifications that poured murderous fire into the Marines. So while some Marines were left on Hill 362-A to prevent its reoccupation, other 28th Marines descended the sloped draw to move up Nishi Ridge. Control of Hill 362-A by the 28th Marines was the key to capturing Nishi Ridge. Before the end of 1 March, three men from the 2nd Battalion, 28th Marines who raised the flags atop Mount Suribachi (Sergeant Michael Strank, Corporal Harlon Block and Sergeant Henry 'Hank' Hansen) were KIA, and a fourth (Corporal Charles Lindberg, a flamethrower) was WIA. (Photo: *Sgt J.T. Dreyfuss*) (NARA)

A Marine bazooka team aims at a Japanese position from a rocky perch during the drive through northern Iwo Jima. Bazookas proved to be an invaluable weapon on rocky hillsides firing pointblank into enemy positions. On 26 February, as the 23rd Marines, 4th Division worked its way through a minefield beside a perimeter track of Airfield No. 2 during an advance towards a ruined radio station at the foot of Hill 382, Private 1st Class Douglas Jacobson picked up a bazooka from a team that had been felled by a Japanese MG. Jacobson then went on to silence sixteen Japanese defensive positions using his bazooka single-handedly until he ran out of ammunition. Over the course of half an hour, Jacobson killed seventy-five Japanese soldiers, and for this, he was awarded the Congressional Medal of Honor. Jacobson had opened a gap in Hill 382's defences to secure a tenuous foothold for an attempt by I Company 23rd Marines to scale the height. After getting to the summit of Hill 382, I Company had to retreat after almost five hours of combat. (Photo: *Sgt L.R. Burmeister*) (*NARA*)

(**Above**) A Marine loads three bazooka rocket launcher tubes suspended from an OY 1 Sentinel light aircraft's wing struts in March, the only armament that was occasionally fitted to the plane. The 'O' indicated observation and 'Y' was the symbol for Convair, which was created in 1943 by the merger of the Consolidated and Vultee companies. The Marines preferred calling these single-engine, high-wing aircraft 'Grasshoppers' as they were originally designed for US Army liaison and artillery spotter duties. On Iwo Jima on 27 February, the Marines began using the captured Airfield No. 1 for OY aircraft, with a 'Grasshopper' becoming the first plane to use the airstrip. (Photo: *Pfc Budd Lindsley*) (*NARA*)

(**Opposite**) USN Grumman F6F Hellcats on a fighter sweep over the rugged terrain of northern Iwo Jima. The Hellcat was designed to replace the earlier Grumman F4F Wildcat and to counter the IJN Mitsubishi A6M Reisen 'Zero'. Wing armament included six 0.50-inch calibre Browning MGs. Each aircraft could carry six 5-inch rockets to attack ground targets. The F6F-5 variant was developed to serve as a fighter-bomber, which could carry up to 2,000lb of bombs or other ordnance. Another variant of the F6F-5 was equipped with harder-hitting 20mm cannons replacing the inner wing MGs. Part of the inadequacy of naval air support was related to the Japanese masterful camouflage of positions and ordnance. After the Marine ground commanders critiqued USN air support, squadrons' performance from the escort carriers improved with use of use of heavier 500lb bombs and quicker sortie response time. Subsequently, Major General Cates, the 4th Division CG, rated the naval air support as 'entirely satisfactory'. After Spruance's fleet carriers departed Iwo's waters, USN and USAAF pilots supported the troops fighting ashore. On 9 March, Iwo-based USAAF P-51s joined carrier planes in strikes against Japanese in the northern tip of the island and continued flying troop support missions until 14 March. (*NARA*)

(**Above**) A USN destroyer shells Japanese positions in northern Iwo with its 5-inch guns to support the VAC drive on 2 March. The Marines valued the continuous and responsive support received from D-Day onwards from naval gunfire frequently less than a mile offshore. Many vessels took hits from Japanese coast defence batteries. Smaller vessels such as modified landing craft with 4.2-inch mortars, rockets or 20mm guns were also invaluable, especially along the north-west coast as they worked in conjunction with the 5th Division as it approached 'The Gorge'. (Photo: *Sgt A.J. Kiely, Jr.*) (*NARA*)

(**Opposite, above**) A Marine M1 155mm howitzer provides direct fire support for an advance in northern Iwo Jima. On 25 February, two battalions of 155mm howitzers (CO Colonel John S. Letcher) came ashore to provide direct fire support to complement requested fire from cruisers and destroyers assigned to each Marine manoeuvring unit. Designed in 1940 and delivered to American forces in 1941, it needed motor vehicle transport. (*NARA*)

(**Opposite, below**) Marines from the 1st Battalion, 26th Marines, 5th Division rest after planting the 'Stars and Stripes' atop Hill 165 near Kitano Point on 19 March (centre, top), three weeks after the initial two flags were raised on Mount Suribachi. The 1st Battalion CO, Lieutenant Colonel Daniel Pollock, was awarded a Navy Cross for heroism in leading his battalion. His citation for action on 19 March read: 'During the fifth consecutive day of combat against strong enemy defenses concealed by camouflage in extremely rough terrain, LC Pollock moved forward into the front lines under intense fire and conducting a thorough personal reconnaissance of this area, prepared a bold enveloping maneuver aimed towards positions behind Hill 165, the last high ground on the island controlled by the Japanese. He increased the morale and fighting efficiency of the battalion by words of encouragement as he proceeded from man to man.' Pollock was evacuated from Iwo Jima due to wounds received during the assault. (Photo: *Pvt R. Campbell*) (*NARA*)

(**Above**) A group of Japanese prisoners in the 3rd Division sector eat rations on 26 March. Evidence of the enemy's resistance to the last was obtained in the numbers of POWs taken: a total of 216 by the VAC, which included Korean labourers. In the 'mopping-up' phase until the end of June, another 867 prisoners were captured with 1,602 of the enemy killed by the US Army's 147th Infantry Regiment, at a cost of 15 soldiers KIA and another 144 WIA. (Photo: *TSgt J. Heiberger*) (*NARA*)

(**Opposite, above**) A Marine flushes out Japanese soldiers from a cave with a hand grenade, with two US Army 147th Infantry Regiment, 37th ('Buckeye') Division soldiers armed with Thompson 0.45-inch calibre SMGs behind him. Almost 3,000 men of the 147th Infantry Regiment landed on Iwo Jima on 21 March. Five days later, most of the victorious Marines left the island, leaving the 'mopping-up' to the 147th Infantry Regiment. Although Marine Intelligence officers estimated only 100–300 Japanese on Iwo, on 26 March, 200–300 enemy soldiers attacked a bivouac area for the Marines set to depart the island. The Marine 5th Pioneer Battalion with the help of Company A, 147th Infantry Regiment, along with a flamethrower tank, blunted the attack. The 147th Infantry Regiment split the island into three sectors and assigned each battalion the task of clearing out the holed-up Japanese by using ambush and combat patrols as well as cave explorations. The soldiers who eliminated the enemy in their excavated positions were called 'Cave Men'. The 147th Infantry Regiment departed Iwo Jima on 8 September, and moved to Okinawa for similar tasks. (*NARA*)

(**Opposite, below**) Japanese Major Masaru Inaoka, senior medical officer of the 2nd Mixed Brigade Hospital, located 100 feet underground in a cave, surrenders on 11 April to a Company A patrol led by Captain James T. Kolb of the 147th Infantry Regiment with the assistance of *Nisei* MIS interpreter Sergeant Ritsuevo Tanaka. Over the next several hours, thirteen Japanese medical officers and fifty-nine enlisted medical troops crawled through the cave's 2-foot-square exit. A few Japanese refused to surrender and committed suicide. (Author's collection)

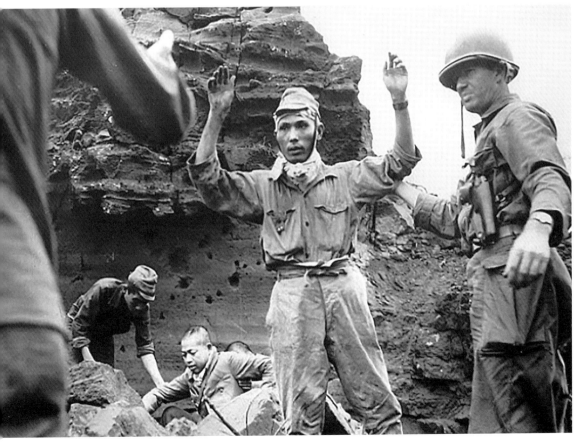

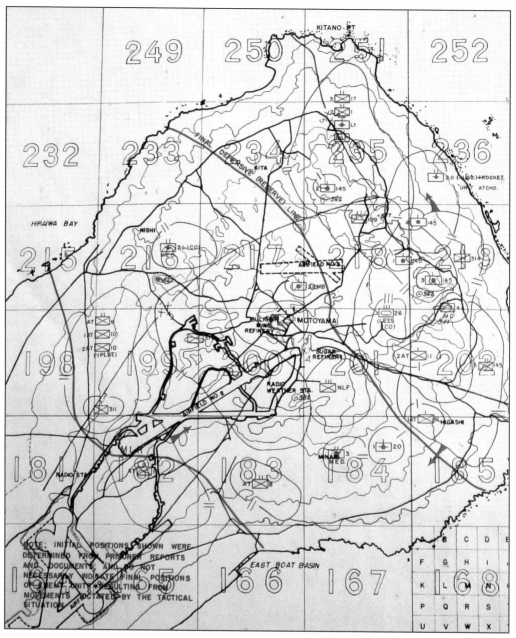

Map of Japanese positions and pivotal terrain landmarks (see text for details) on northern Iwo Jima from Airfield No. 2 to Kitano Point. After Mount Suribachi's fall, Kuribayashi still had 8 infantry battalions, a tank regiment, 2 artillery and 3 heavy mortar battalions in addition to 5,000 artillerymen and IJN infantry under Rear Admiral Toshinosuke Ichimaru. Colonel Chosaku Kaido, Chief of Artillery, was in charge of the reinforced concrete blockhouse on 'Turkey Knob', a ridge in the east-central sector of the Motoyama Plateau. Major General Sadasue Senda commanded the 2nd IMB, which would fight the 4th Division over a twenty-five-day interval. The 204th Naval Construction Battalion built a system of hundreds of caves and tunnels in northern Iwo Jima. One cave had a tunnel 800 feet long with fourteen separate exits. Some Marines quipped that the Japanese were not on Iwo Jima but rather in it due to their extensive pre-invasion tunnelling efforts. (*NARA*)

Chapter Six

The Flag Raising atop Mount Suribachi, 23 February 1945

On the morning of 23 February, Lieutenant Colonel Chandler W. Johnson, CO, 2nd Battalion, 28th Marines, sent a forty-man reinforced 3rd Platoon, Company E, led by 1st Lieutenant Harold G. Schrier, to climb the north face of Mount Suribachi, reach its peak, and hoist the American flag on the volcano's rim after an earlier four-man patrol of Company F, led by Sergeant Sherman B. Watson, similarly did so without encountering the enemy or hearing noise from caves, tunnels, destroyed blockhouses and pillboxes from the previous naval bombardment. Within a few hours, Marine combat photographer Staff Sergeant Louis Lowery of *Leatherneck* magazine photographed the first flag raising atop the mountain. Marine combat cinematographer Sergeant William Genaust made a 16mm photograph of the iconic second flag raising, which was simultaneously captured on film by Wartime Still Picture Pool photographer for Associated Press, Joe Rosenthal. Other combat photographers taking several images each to memorialize the event included Marine Private Bob Campbell, Marine Sergeant Louis R. Burmeister and US Army combat photographer for *YANK* magazine, Private George Burns. Secretary of the Navy James Forrestal turned to Lieutenant General Holland M. Smith, the Joint Expeditionary Force CG, and said, 'Holland, the raising of that flag on Suribachi means a Marine Corps for the next 500 years.'

Of the forty-man patrol responsible for the first flag raising, thirty-six were KIA or WIA in later fighting.

(**Above**) Aerial view of Mount Suribachi's crater at Iwo Jima's southern tip looking south-west to north-east, with landing ships at the eastern beaches. The 28th Marines who raised the two flags on 23 February ascended the mountain's north face. (*NARA*)

(**Opposite, above**) Members of a Marine patrol at the apex of Mount Suribachi's north face call Lieutenant Colonel Chandler Johnson at his 2nd Battalion, 28th Marines CP at the volcano's base to tell him that the summit was secure. The Marines atop the summit were told to raise the first flag on the morning of 23 February. (Photo: *SSgt L. Lowery*) (Leatherneck *magazine / NARA*)

(**Opposite, below**) On the morning of 23 February, 1st Lieutenant Harold G. Schrier (left), Platoon Sergeant Ernest Thomas, Jr. (middle), Corporal Charles Lindberg, a flamethrower and leader of the 3rd Platoon Assault Squad (right), all of the 3rd Platoon, Company E, 2nd Battalion, 28th Marines, led by Schrier (Company XO), lash a 54-inch by 28-inch flag from the transport USS *Missoula*, which was brought ashore by the 2nd Battalion, 28th Marines adjutant, Lieutenant George G. Wells, to a 20-foot section of Japanese pipe found near the crater's north rim. Lieutenant Colonel Chandler W. Johnson (CO 2nd Battalion, 28th Marines) dispatched twenty-five Marines, but Schrier added another fifteen men to reinforce the platoon before starting the ascent to secure the crater's rim for the flag raising. Passing apparently deserted cave entrances and dead Japanese, the Marine detail pressed on to positions along the inside of the rim of the volcanic crater thirty minutes after leaving the 2nd Battalion, 28th Marines' informal CP to thrust the American flag into soft ground at 1020 hours. Schrier and Lindberg were both previously Marine Raiders like the 28th Marines CO, Colonel Harry Liversedge. Platoon Sergeant Ernest J. Thomas, Jr., who met with Lieutenant General Holland M. Smith aboard the command ship *Eldorado* on 24 February, was KIA on 3 March. Other platoons soon joined the Schrier patrol at the summit and began to help with the crater's 'mopping-up'. Lieutenant Colonel Johnson quickly decided to replace the first flag with a larger one (96 inches by 56 inches) obtained from LST *779*, beached near Suribachi's eastern base. (Photo: *SSgt L. Lowery*) (Leatherneck *magazine / NARA*)

(**Above**) 1st Lieutenant Harold Schrier (seated left, on phone) and some of his Marine detail at 1020 hours stand beside the newly raised first flag fluttering in the wind. At left, wearing a radio, is Private 1st Class Raymond Jacobs. Holding the flagpole to its left wearing a soft cap is Sergeant Henry 'Hank' Hansen, a former Marine Paratrooper. Above Hansen's hand holding the upper flagstaff is Pharmacist's Mate 2nd Class John Bradley while beneath Hansen's grip, the lower portion of the flagpole was held by Private Philip Ward. Platoon Sergeant Ernest Thomas, Jr., is seated next to Bradley, a Navy corpsman assigned to Company E, while in the foreground, Private 1st Class James Michels guards against any Japanese lurking nearby with his M1 carbine semi-automatic rifle. Standing above Michels is Corporal Charles Lindberg. (Photo: *SSgt L. Lowery*) (Leatherneck *magazine / NARA*)

(**Below**) Some of the 3rd Platoon, Company E, 2nd Battalion, 28th Marines that raised the first flag on Mount Suribachi during the late morning hours of 23 February. From left to right are: Corporal Charles Lindberg, Sergeant Howard Snyder, Pharmacist's Mate 2nd Class John Bradley, Private Philip Ward, Platoon Sergeant Ernest Thomas, Jr., Sgt Henry 'Hank' Hansen, Private 1st Class Ray Jacobs, radioman, and 1st Lieutenant Harold G. Schrier, seated using radio to report the flag raising to Lieutenant Colonel Chandler, Johnson's CP. (Photo: *SSgt L. Lowery*) (Leatherneck *magazine / USMC*)

(**Above**) Some 2nd Battalion, 28th Marines rest after the first flag raising atop Suribachi on the morning of 23 February. Private 1st Class Louis Charlo (foreground), a member of the Bitteroot Salish (or Flathead) Native-American Indian tribe from Montana, enlisted in the USMC in 1944 and was one of four members of Company F, 2nd Battalion, 28th Marines' 'Watson reconnaissance patrol'. Charlo died during a company advance on 2 March as he tried to rescue wounded Marines. (Photo: *Sgt L.R. Burmeister*) (*NARA*)

(**Opposite**) Marine Staff Sergeant Louis R. Lowery, a 29-year-old Pittsburgh, Pennsylvania native, was a newspaper photographer for the Pittsburgh *Post Dispatch* before enlisting, and became a Marine staff photographer for *Leatherneck* magazine attached to the 5th Division. He holds his camera by a rock pile and Japanese sandbags atop Mount Suribachi in front of the smaller (54-inch by 28-inch) first flag raised at 1020 hours on 23 February and immortalized in his photographs. Lowery was the only Marine combat photographer to cover six major Pacific campaigns (Peleliu, Saipan, Tinian, Guam, Iwo Jima and Okinawa). On the morning of 23 February, Staff Sergeant Lowery accompanied and photographed the forty-man combat patrol climb to Mount Suribachi's summit to seize the volcano's rim in order to raise the first flag signalling its capture to American forces below. Soon after the flag raising, two Japanese charged Lowery from a cave near the summit. One enemy soldier was killed while waving his samurai sword while the other threw a hand grenade at Lowery, who jumped over the rim to slide down the mountain 50 feet to avoid death or injury. Other Japanese, in response to the flag raising came out of their caves near the crater only to be killed by the Marines. Lowery's camera was smashed but the negatives remained intact to memorialize the initial hoisting of the smaller flag from the USS *Missoula*. His only other camera was destroyed when he landed on the beach thirty minutes after H-Hour with the 5th Division on 19 February. No other photographer came up until after the first flag was raised and Lowery got the 'scoop'. When Lowery descended from the summit in search of a new camera, he stopped to speak with Joe Rosenthal, Sergeant William Genaust, and Private Bob Campbell, who were trekking up the mountain. Lowery's film shots, like Campbell's (pp. 210, 213–15) as well as Genaust's movie (p. 211) were handled by mail and none of it was developed until it reached the United States. On the other hand, Rosenthal's film went to Guam on a courier flying boat for development and cropping of the original horizontal photograph into a dramatic vertical image (p. 212) showing a solid 'pyramid of Marines beneath the rising national colors'. Lowery remained in the USMC Reserve after the war, obtaining a rank of captain. He also served as the president of the Marine Corps Correspondents Association and became photographic director of *Leatherneck* magazine. He was the recipient of two Purple Heart Medals. (Photo: *SSgt M.A. Cornelius*) (Author's collection)

Marines examine Mount Suribachi through a captured Japanese field scope on 23 February. To the right of the Marine using the field scope is Marine cinematographer Sergeant William Genaust (holding cigarette) of Sioux Falls, South Dakota, who would make a colour 16mm film of the second flag raising later that afternoon simultaneous with the iconic Joe Rosenthal Still photograph and many other images made by Marine Private Bob Campbell. Genaust served in the Pacific and was awarded the Bronze Star and Purple Heart medals for his combat role in a firefight on Saipan, where he was wounded on 9 July 1944. It took eight months for Genaust to recover from his leg wound and although he was offered to return home, he instead volunteered to go to Iwo Jima, landing on 19 February. On 22 February, he teamed with 5th Marine Division photographer Private Bob Campbell to take film action at the base of Mount Suribachi. After the initial flag raising, around noon on 23 February, Sergeant Genaust and Private Campbell were ordered to go up Mount Suribachi, where they met Associated Press photographer Joe Rosenthal. (Photo: *Pvt R. Campbell*) (NARA)

Three representative frames from Sergeant William Genaust's 16mm film of the second flag raising at the volcano's summit after Lieutenant Colonel Chandler Johnson, the 2nd Battalion, 28th Marines CO, sent a Marine to the summit with a second flag from LST *779* that was twice as large. The new flag was immediately tied to a longer length of pipe and six Marines planted the new flagstaff into the rubble atop the summit. (Photo: *Sgt William Genaust*) (*NARA*)

The legendary Joe Rosenthal photograph of the second flag raising atop Suribachi's summit is shown here. Rosenthal landed on D-Day with the 4th Marine Division and returned to the USS *Eldorado* each night to compose captions for his photographs and to ensure that his negatives were aboard the courier flying boat to Guam. Rosenthal's image, called the war's most memorable photograph, won the 1945 Pulitzer Prize and became the official symbol of the 7th War Bond Drive, during which $220 million in bonds were sold. The image was reproduced on a US postage stamp and was the reference for the world's largest bronze statue at the foot of Arlington National Cemetery in Virginia. (Photo: *Associated Press photographer Joe Rosenthal*) (*NARA*)

When Lieutenant Colonel Chandler Johnson (CO 2nd Battalion, 28th Marines) witnessed how the Marines responded to the first flag being raised, he ordered a second, larger flag from LST 779 to be raised in its place. Lieutenant Ted Tuttle of the 2nd Battalion, 28th Marines' operations staff procured the larger flag, 96 inches by 56 inches, by talking to a USN ensign aboard LST 779, who retrieved the larger flag from a locker at Pearl Harbor's Salvage Depot. Under Lieutenant Schrier's orders, the second larger flag from the Genaust film and Rosenthal image replaced the first smaller flag from the Lowery photograph as it was lowered simultaneously. Private Bob Campbell captured both flags with his Speed Graphic camera for black-and-white still images. (Photo: *Pvt R. Campbell*) (*NARA*)

1st Lieutenant Harold G. Schrier (left), the 3rd Platoon, Company E, 2nd Battalion, 28th Marines leader who ordered the second, larger flag to be installed once it arrived from LST *779*, and Platoon Sergeant Ernest 'Boots' Thomas (right) salute the flag after it had been planted by the six Marines in the iconic Genaust film and Rosenthal photograph and held in place as other Marines searched for ties to anchor the flag against the winds atop Mount Suribachi. (Photo: *Pvt R. Campbell*) *(NARA)*

Joe Rosenthal (right) standing atop a Japanese sandbag on stones for elevation and Sergeant William Genaust, kneeling with his motion picture camera (left), as they take the image of the 28th Marines comprising the famous Rosenthal 'Gung Ho' photograph from the rim of Mount Suribachi. (Photo: *Pvt R. Campbell*) (*NARA*)

Wartime Still Picture Pool Associated Press Photographer Joe Rosenthal (left) and Army Private George Burns, a combat photographer for *YANK* magazine, atop Mount Suribachi after the second flag raising on 23 February. *(USAHEC)*

Sergeant Howard Snyder (left) and Corporal Harold Keller pose between the first and second flag raisings atop Mount Suribachi. Both Marines were among the first of Lieutenant Harold Schrier's platoon to reach the summit that morning. (Photo: *Pvt G. Burns*)
(YANK *magazine / USAHEC*)

The contingent of Company E, 2nd Battalion, 28th Marines just after the Rosenthal 'Gung Ho' photograph. They appear nonchalant although some Japanese snipers were present and still lurking in caves. (Photo: *Pvt G. Burns*) (YANK *magazine / USAHEC*)

Two Marines stare northward from the second flag raised atop Mount Suribachi. (Photo: *SSgt M. Kauffman*) (*NARA*)

Private Philip Ward hangs a Japanese Rising Sun flag (*Yosegaki Hinomaru*) at Mount Suribachi's zenith with the USN invasion armada (background). (Photo: *Pvt G. Burns*) (YANK *magazine / USAHEC*)

Marine cinematographers Sergeant William Genaust (left) and Corporal Atlee S. Tracey (right) in a captured Japanese shelter on 24 February, the day after the flag raisings on Mount Suribachi. Unfortunately, Genaust never saw his cinematic 16mm footage as he was deemed MIA on 3 March and ruled KIA the next day as he was filming Marines in combat clearing caves and tunnels during the battle for Hill 382. An account of Genaust's death is that he and an interpreter, a Marine lieutenant, volunteered to enter a cave to speak with a Japanese soldier sitting at a table. As the pair of Marines was two-thirds of the way into the cave, Genaust was shot by an MG in a concealed entrance. The lieutenant ordered the cave mouth to be sealed with a demolition charge and Genaust's body was buried in the blast. The Marine officer deemed that more men would have been killed in carrying out Genaust's body as the Japanese moved deeper into the cave with no intent to surrender. Genaust joined the Marines in Minnesota and served with HQ Company, 5th Division as a photographer for Division Intelligence. Tracey worked with Genaust at the Photography Section, Motion Pictures, in the 5th Division. (Photo: *Pvt R. Campbell*) (*NARA*)

Associated Press photographer Joe Rosenthal (left) and Private Bob Campbell (right), Marine combat photographer assigned to the 5th Division, sit at the base of Mount Suribachi on 2 March in front of a destroyed Japanese casemate housing a piece of heavy ordnance. Campbell's own account of the combat on Iwo Jima: 'The enemy here lived almost completely underground and in spacious subterranean rooms and tunnels. All the rocky slopes and ledges were pitted with gun emplacements with access to tunnels in the rear. That should give you an idea of what we were up against.' Joe Rosenthal, part of the Wartime Pool of Still Photographers, worked as a civilian photographer for the Associated Press and won a Pulitzer Prize and everlasting fame for his still photograph of the second flag raising on Mount Suribachi on 23 February. Private Bob Campbell was born in Oakland, California, in 1910 and shared a darkroom with Rosenthal at the *San Francisco Chronicle* before the war. Campbell also worked at the *Oakland Tribune* and *Oakland Post-Enquirer*. He was drafted into the Army soon after the Pearl Harbor attack, but decided to enlist in the Marine Corps instead (although he had four children at the time of his being drafted) and was attached to the 5th Division, taking innumerable photographs of the Iwo Jima campaign. (*Author's collection*)

An unidentified Marine combat photographer takes an image of a burning Marine M4 tank hit by a Japanese shell in northern Iwo Jima. More than fifty Marine combat cameramen operated across Iwo Jima during the battle from 19 February to 26 March. Many shot still images, but at least twenty-six made motion pictures. Three of the twenty-six cinematographers were KIA, including the 5th Division's Sergeant William Genaust. Private 1st Class Don Fox, a 5th Division combat photographer, also perished. (Photo: *Cpl E. Jones*) (*NARA*)

Army Private George Burns (left) providing combat photographs for *YANK* magazine sits at a beachhead with a shore party member as reinforcements arrive. (*USAHEC*)

5th Division combat photographer Sergeant David Christian gets a head wound dressed by Navy corpsman Pharmacist's Mate 1st Class Hubert Hammond in a rocky crevice after being WIA on 24 February. Christian was also wounded on 1 March, and received a Purple Heart. (Photo: *Sgt R. Follendorf*) (*NARA*)

Sergeant David Christian, a 5th Division combat photographer who was wounded earlier that day, 24 February, wears his head bandage and carries an M1 carbine near a destroyed Japanese Kawasaki Ki-45 twin-engine, two-seat fighter ('Gekko') at Airfield No. 1. (*NARA*)

Staff Sergeant Norm Hatch (right) at his 5th Division Photo Section, which he supervised on Iwo Jima with Warrant Officer Obie Newcomb, Jr., USMCR, the 5th Division assistant photography officer (left). Hatch and Newcomb landed with the 5th Division's first wave on 19 February. Hatch joined the Marine Corps in 1939 and served as a combat photographer on Guadalcanal, Tarawa and Iwo Jima. Hatch filmed the Academy Award-winning 1944 short documentary *With the Marines at Tarawa* as a combat photographer with the 2nd Division, under the leadership of Marine Captain Louis Hayward, a Hollywood film star and 2nd Division photographic officer. On the morning of 23 February, Hatch ordered his 5th Division subordinates, Sergeant William Genaust and Private Bob Campbell, to join the Marine detachment heading up Mount Suribachi with the second, larger flag for the second raising that afternoon. On Iwo, Warrant Officer Newcomb documented the amphibious landings, ground assaults and combat of individual Marine and small groups as well the treatment of wounded Marines by USN doctors and corpsmen. (Photo: *SSgt M.A. Cornelius*) (*NARA*)

Photographers Corporal Eugene S. Jones from the Washington *Times Herald* and his twin brother, Private 1st Class Charles O. Jones, now with VAC but formerly with the Washington *Daily News*, are reunited on Iwo Jima in February. (*NARA*)

Marine 5th Division combat photographer Corporal Richard H. Stotz holds his camera on 14 March. Stotz enlisted in December 1942, and in 1944 was assigned to the 28th Marines, 5th Division in an Intelligence Platoon as a motion and still picture photographer. After additional photography training, he rejoined his platoon with fellow photographer Sergeant Louis R. Burmeister. Throughout the Pacific War, he amassed four binders of nearly 1,200 photographs, including the 5th Division Marines landing at Green Beach, Navy corpsmen aiding the wounded, and innumerable others. (Photo: *Pvt R. Campbell*) (*NARA*)

USCG combat photographer Charles W. Bossert landed at Iwo Jima with three cameras, none of which survived the campaign. Two disappeared skyward when enemy mortar fire landed on the spot where Bossert placed them. Under hellacious Japanese fire, Bossert burrowed into a volcanic ash foxhole with his remaining camera; however, shrapnel from a nearby Japanese shell tore a jagged hole through the centre of the camera. (*NARA*)

Sergeant Albert R. Morejohn, a Cuban-American and 4th Division combat photographer, enlisted in the Marine Corps after graduating from high school in New York City. He posed with his 0.45-inch calibre 1911 semi-automatic pistol holstered on his right hip. (*Author's collection*)

USN Captain Edward J. Steichen (right) on Iwo Jima with a Marine corporal. During the Second World War, he was director of the USN Photographic Institute. In 1944, he directed the war documentary *The Fighting Lady*, which won an Academy Award for Best Documentary Feature. He also curated an exhibition in January 1945, *Power in the Pacific: Battle Photographs of our Navy in Action on the Sea and in the Sky*. A photograph of Steichen above the USS *Lexington*'s flight deck in November 1943 appears outside of NARA II's Still Picture Room in College Park, Maryland. (*NARA*)

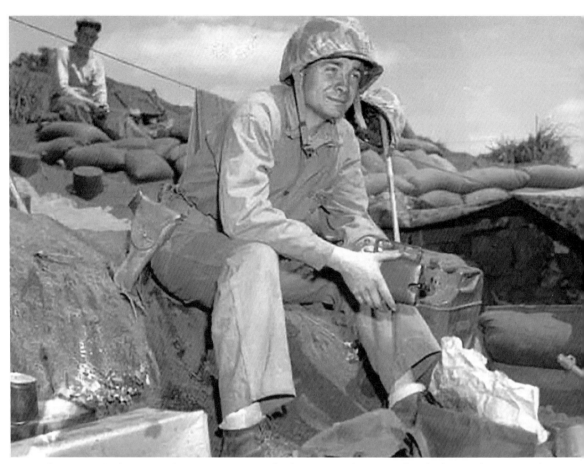

Sergeant Arthur J. Kiely, Jr., was a *Hartford Courant* photographer before enlisting in the Marine Corps as a combat photographer. He served with the 3rd and 4th Divisions on Guam and Saipan, respectively, and was awarded a Bronze Star when, as a corporal, he killed at least three Japanese soldiers during a Marianas Island battle, after putting down his camera. Kiely was brought onto Lieutenant General Holland M. Smith's staff (Fleet Marine Force, Pacific, Public Relations), where he took many photographs of Smith. (*Author's collection*)

Epilogue

In the thirty-six days of combat on Iwo Jima, VAC killed approximately 22,000 Japanese soldiers and sailors. The Marines captured only 216 Japanese troops as the island was finally declared secured on 26 March. The Marines and USN personnel suffered 24,053 casualties, the highest single action loss in Marine Corps history. Of these, 6,140 died. Astonishingly, one Marine or Navy corpsman became a casualty for every three Americans that landed on the island. Stated by another metric, 700 Americans died for every square mile seized. The decimation among the ranks of assault infantry in platoon, company and battalion strengths was brutal. The number of casualties among officers was also staggering, as exemplified by Company B, 1st Battalion, 28th Marines, 5th Division losing nine company commanders in combat.

After bloody combat amid the volcanic ash of the beachhead and entrenched Japanese positions, especially at Mount Suribachi, the 4th and 5th Divisions disembarked on 19 and 26 March, respectively. On 7 April, eighty P-51 fighters from USAAF 7th Fighter Command flew from Iwo Jima escorting a B-29 attack on the Nakajima aircraft engine factory in Tokyo. Iwo Jima had to be seized for the successful strategic bombing campaign of Japan's Home Islands. When the war had ended, a total of 24,761 American airmen were rescued when 2,251 B-29s made emergency landings at Iwo Jima. In fact, the initial B-29 emergency landing on Iwo Jima was on 4 March. If not for the valiant Marines' sacrifice to capture the island, many of those airmen would have died. For their gallantry, twenty-seven Congressional Medals of Honor were awarded – the largest number won by Marines in one battle (22), Navy Corpsmen (4), and one USN landing craft commander – representing over 25 per cent of the eighty Medals of Honor awarded to Marines during the Second World War. The Medal of Honor recipients' names, photographs and heroic circumstances of their sacrifice are listed in Appendix VIII of the US Marine Corps' *Iwo Jima: Amphibious Epic* by Lieutenant Colonel Whitman S. Bartley, USMC.

(**Above**) A 3rd Division Marine in full battle kit lies dead at a sand terrace's top clutching his bayonet, with his M1 Garand rifle nearby. (Photo: *Sgt D.R. Francis*) (*NARA*)

(**Opposite, above**) The bodies of deceased 3rd Division Marines lie under their ponchos as Marine burial parties check identification and personal possessions on 28 February, with the vast USN armada in the background. (Photo: *Cpl R. Impenachio*) (*NARA*)

(**Opposite, below**) Chaplain Wood, the 4th Division chaplain, conducts a burial at sea of a deceased 4th Division Marine with a honour guard behind him on a USCG-crewed transport, which served as a floating hospital, on 22 February. (Photo: *Pfc Budd Lindsley*) (*NARA*)

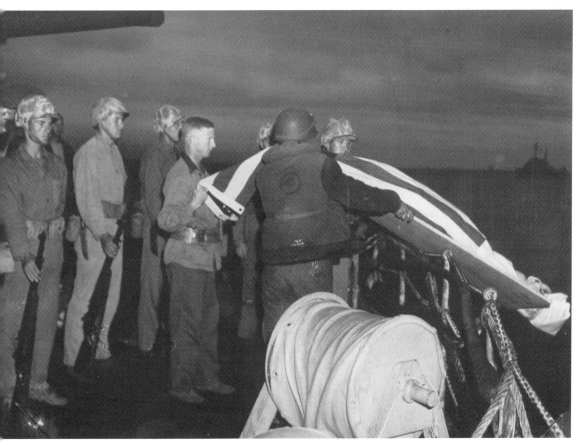

(**Opposite, above**) The 5th Division cemetery with the American flag flying amid neat rows of crosses and Mount Suribachi looming (background). (*NARA*)

(**Opposite, below**) The hand of a dead Japanese soldier buried under rock rubble and dirt after he was killed in a bomb blast. (Photo: *Capt E.J. Steichen*) (*NARA*)

(**Above**) Private 1st Class Robert Conover, 25th Marines, 4th Division, who survived the hellacious campaign, cleans his captured Japanese officer's pistol as he prepares to board an LST to leave Sulphur Island as a survivor of the ordeal. (Photo: *TSgt H.N. Gillespie*) (*NARA*)

Two riflemen from 1st Battalion, 26th Marines move up past a comrade's grave marked by a rifle and a helmet, 28 February. (Photo: *Pfc C. Jones*) (*NARA*)

P-51 Mustangs of the USAAF 7th Fighter Command are parked on Airfield No. 1 with a B-29 Superfortress (background) as they prepare to continue the aerial war against the Japanese Home Islands, a primary reason for the amphibious invasion of Iwo Jima and the protracted thirty-six-day campaign. (*NARA*)

Bibliography

Alexander, J.H., *Closing In: Marines in the Seizure of Iwo Jima* (CreateSpace Independent Publishing Platform, Orlando, 2024).

Bartley, W.S., *Iwo Jima: Amphibious Epic* (US Govt Printing Office, Washington, 1954).

Conner, H. & Rockey, K., *The Spearhead: The World War II History of the 5th Marine Division* (Infantry Journal Press, Washington, 1950).

Costello, J., *The Pacific War 1941–1945* (Quill, New York, 1982).

Gailey, H.A., *The War in the Pacific: From Pearl Harbor to Tokyo Bay* (Presidio Press, Novato, 1995).

Garand, G.W. & Strobridge, T.R., *Western Pacific Operations. History of the U.S. Marine Corps in World War II. Volume IV* (Historical Division, Headquarters, US Marine Corps, Washington, 1971).

Hammel, E., *Iwo Jima* (Zenith Press, St. Paul, 2006).

Hammel, E., *Two Flags over Iwo Jima: Solving the Mystery of the U.S. Marine Corps' Proudest Moment* (Casemate Publishers, Philadelphia, 2018).

Hastings, M., *Retribution: The Battle for Japan, 1944–45* (Vintage Books, New York, 2009).

Jones, C., *War Shots: Norm Hatch and the U.S. Marine Corps Combat Cameramen of World War II* (Stackpole Books, Mechanicsburg, 2011).

Khan, M., *Images of War. The Battle of Iwo Jima: Raising the Flag, February–March 1945* (Frontline Books, Yorkshire and Philadelphia, 2018).

Leckie, R., *Strong Men Armed: The United States Marines against Japan* (Bantam Books, New York, 1963).

Leckie, R., *Delivered from Evil: The Saga of World War II* (Harper Perennial, New York, 1988).

Marston, D., *The Pacific War Companion: From Pearl Harbor to Hiroshima* (Osprey, Oxford, 2005).

McNaughton, J.C., *Nisei Linguists: Japanese Americans in the Military Intelligence Service during World War II* (Department of the Army, Washington, 2006.)

Newcomb, R.F., *Iwo Jima: The Dramatic Account of the Epic Battle that Turned the Tide of World War II* (Henry Holt and Company, New York, 1965).

Ross, B.D., *Iwo Jima: Legacy of Valor* (Vintage Books, New York, 1985).

Simmons, E.H., *The United States Marines: The First Two Hundred Years 1775–1975* (Viking Press, New York, 1976).

Spector, R.H., *Eagle Against the Sun: The American War with Japan* (Vintage Books, New York, 1985).

Wheeler, R., *A Special Valor: The U.S. Marines and the Pacific War* (Castle Books, Edison, 1996).

Wheeler, R., *The Bloody Battle of Suribachi* (Skyhorse Publishing, New York, 2007).

Wright, D., *Iwo Jima 1945: The Marines Raise the Flag on Mount Suribachi* (Osprey, Oxford, 2001).

Dear Reader,

We hope you have enjoyed this book, but why not share your views on social media? You can also follow our pages to see more about our other products: facebook.com/penandswordbooks or follow us on X @penswordbooks

You can also view our products at www.pen-and-sword.co.uk (UK and ROW) or www.penandswordbooks.com (North America).

To keep up to date with our latest releases and online catalogues, please sign up to our newsletter at: www.pen-and-sword.co.uk/newsletter

If you would like a printed catalogue with our latest books, then please email: enquiries@pen-and-sword.co.uk or telephone: 01226 734555 (UK and ROW) or email: uspen-and-sword@casematepublishers.com or telephone: (610) 853-9131 (North America).

We respect your privacy and we will only use personal information to send you information about our products.

Thank you!